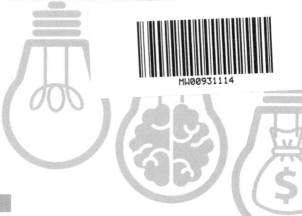

MW00931114

THE
STARTUP
INVESTOR
MINDSET

A guide to discovering the top ways to influence, catalyze innovation & impact early-stage ventures as an investor

DR. SILVIA MAH

THE STARTUP INVESTOR MINDSET

A guide to discovering the top ways to influence, catalyze innovation & impact early-stage ventures as an investor

Copyright © 2023 by Dr. Silvia Mah

All rights reserved. No part of this publication may be reproduced, stored in a retrieval system, or transmitted in any form or by any means electronically, mechanically, photocopying, recording, or otherwise, without the prior written permission of the publisher except in the case of brief quotations embodied in critical articles and reviews.

DISCLAIMER

Early-stage investment is the riskiest asset class to grow personal wealth. Startups are a risky endeavor. Any investor funding these types of businesses is taking on incredible risk, so I encourage investors to balance their personal wealth portfolio with less risky asset classes.

Dedication

To my mother, the feminist who raised me and who still encourages my curiosity, deepens my resolve, and strengthens my integrity.
I am loved.

To my children, my everything, I do all of this for you.
I am blessed.

To my husband, who respects me for the quirky academic he married.
I am accepted.

To the women who stood before me in defiance and solidarity, to the women who continue to hype others, empower through action, and respect each other's uniqueness.
I am grateful.

Contents

Owning the Mindset for a Purposeful Investor Journey

Welcome to crafting a mindset about impactful startup investing at the earliest stages of a brilliant startup's journey. I am so excited to bring this value to you as an experienced early-stage investor from an angel investor and venture capitalist perspective. Writing this book was inspired by many conversations I have had with aspiring investors on how to start thinking like an investor, acting like an investor, and influencing their ecosystem. This topic is also highly influenced by the entrepreneurs I have invested in, advised, or mentored when they dream about being an investor when they exit or ask me how investors think. These insights inform their tactical approaches to investors during their fundraising periods. Mindset matters for intentional and purposeful investing by derisking fears, building a thoughtful thesis, embracing an investor's growth mindset within an industry of great uncertainty, and the list goes on. I hope to be able to gift this tactical and mindful guide to engaged investors, curious entrepreneurs, and thoughtful innovation ecosystem builders who ask introspective questions first before writing a check, asking for a check, or facilitating the connection towards a check, respectively. Here is where their journey begins.

FIND
the
JOY
in the
JOURNEY

The other reason I am excited about writing this book is because my journey as an investor has been full of joy, blessings, and reward that now, after over a decade of investing, I find has been extremely rewarding. When I see and hear other aspiring investors, albeit serial entrepreneurs, lawyers, corporate leaders, or philanthropists, wanting to start their funders' journey, I want them to find the joy in the journey. I want them to love it as much as I do. Here is my attempt to do that.

Learning is a multi-faceted adventure. As investors, the path toward funding exceptional startups initiates and evolves through acquiring knowledge, actively participating in the process, and gaining invaluable experience by taking action. To facilitate this transformative investor journey, this book delves into a helpful framework of factors to acquire valuable insights, amplify traction in your portfolios, and fortify your mindset. The 10-characteristic framework is explored along the outline of the entire book, in between the lines, in the recommendations towards action, and within the figures and tables illustrating key points. (See Figure 1 – The Startup Investor Mindset Framework)

Before delving into the book's content, I encourage you to assess your current engagement with these characteristics. Take a moment to reflect on how well you are embarking on your journey (Present). Once you've read and implemented the actionable steps outlined in the book, I suggest you reassess your approach to investing (Future). By doing so, you'll be able to witness the growth and impact of your investment path toward a thriving portfolio and, hopefully, witness positive changes in your investment strategies and outcomes. Continuous reassessment enables the identification of gaps, thereby facilitating targeted and ongoing growth.

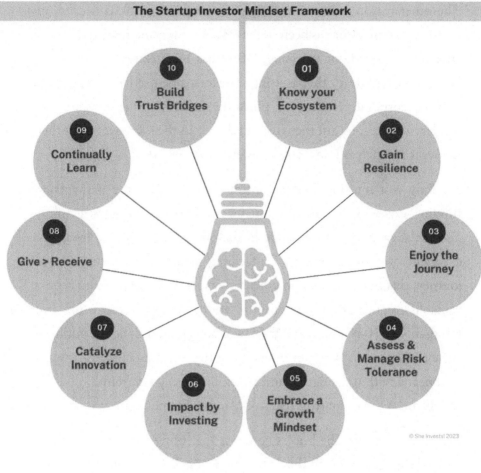

Figure 1

To engage in active learning, let's employ a scale of 0-10 to evaluate your level of embodiment of the top characteristics of an ideal startup investor. Within this range, 0 (zero) denotes the starting point of awareness, whereas 10 (ten) symbolizes the embodiment of a purposeful startup investor, as demonstrated here:

Feel free to fill in the columns in the table on the following page with the appropriate number between 0 and 10 for each of these characteristics both in the present and the future based on your self-assessment.

Characteristics of The Startup Investor Mindset Framework	Present	Future
1. Know Your Ecosystem (Engage in a thriving startup community)		
2. Gain Resilience (Rolling up sleeves and getting feet wet in startups)		
3. Enjoy the Journey (Positive posture toward startup investing)		
4. Assess & Manage Risk Tolerance (Know your guardrails)		
5. Embrace a Growth Mindset (Abundance posture)		
6. Impact by Investing (Write the check, send the wire)		
7. Catalyze Innovation (Source & evaluate innovators)		
8. Give > Receive (Give more than you Receive)		
9. Continually Learn (Investor knowledge acquisition)		
10. Build Trust Bridges (Investors, entrepreneurs & ecosystem builders alike)		
Score as a Collective Startup Investor Mindset (add 1 → 10)	%	%

A brief background about myself: I am a scientist turned academic turned startup advocate turned entrepreneur and eventually an angel investor and venture capitalist. I fell in love with innovation, how it fuels our economy, and how investors can play a critical role in this creation. Entrenched in the startup scene, sourcing, identifying, supporting, investing, and championing the underestimated founder, products, industries, and investors is what I find most invigorating because of the extraordinary amount of research, conversations, and insights needed to make very informed decisions of my portfolio growth (from investors I back as an IC (Investment Committee) or LP (Limited Partner) to the entrepreneurs I fund). Originally from Caracas, Venezuela, I believe in integrating family and work to create a lifestyle that serves both with a strong cup of integrity. Coffee meetings with investors and entrepreneurs alike bring me even more joy.

This book isn't necessarily a guide to read cover to cover. Instead, it's about picking up where you want to begin your journey, where your curiosity takes you along your journey, or where you left off. You might be thinking one morning that you haven't written your investment thesis yet. Well, dive into that section and get it done. After a networking event, you might be wondering what other individuals or organizations you need to connect with in your local startup community, so you can dive into the startup ecosystem map and identify some individuals who are hubs of knowledge, and either meet with them, connect with them on LinkedIn to gain their wisdom. And during those times of guilt, wonder, amazement, or doubt, just flip through this guide to glimpse at quotes to hype you up, gain grounding or enhance perspective. I want to emphasize the importance of a well-informed, healthy, and expansive mindset in the ultimate journey of a startup investor.

This book will not give you every little detail about a startup investor's philosophy and much less the startup investor's journey, tactics, and process. I'm genuinely here to deliver the most concise investor mindset guide to help investors gain clarity on their nascent or ongoing investor career and enjoy that journey. The book explores the significance of confidence, influence, experience, impact, patience, education, empathy, and grace in making informed investment decisions and navigating the challenges of the uncertain and volatile startup ecosystem. Investors equipped with a healthy mindset and joyful disposition will be better prepared to handle exits or non-exits more effectively.

If you find yourself still seated at your desk, it's time to step out and actively engage with entrepreneurs. Take the opportunity to have coffee with experienced investors and fellow enthusiasts. Embracing the spirit of lean startup and design thinking, break free from the routine of your day-to-day activities and find delight in exploring the ever-evolving landscape of innovation. Adopt the thrill of investment with whole-hearted enthusiasm as you immerse yourself in the dynamic world of startups while laying the foundation for generational wealth.

GET COMFY WITH RISK

Chapter 1

Understanding the Startup Investing Landscape

The startup investor mindset embodies a unique way of thinking that profoundly influences the commercialization of innovation. It involves a keen willingness to embrace experimentation and growth, coupled with a posture of perpetual learning and development.

Investors come from multiple different careers and journeys. I've seen lawyers become investors. I've seen serial entrepreneurs become investors after their exit. I have witnessed corporate leaders becoming genuinely excited when they realize they have the opportunity to become investors, then becoming equipped to invest, and then feel comfortable enough investing a small amount of money into early-stage companies within their long-established industries. The fulfillment of this progression is exciting to be a part of. These investors bring exceptional expertise to the founding team, combining their financial support with valuable insights and guidance, making their investment all the more valuable. I've seen philanthropists who want to activate their capital differently in a new asset class go into early-stage investment as a diversification strategy. As an investor, there are so many ways to impact a community, then impact a market, and finally, impact an entire economy.

The innovation economy is built from bright minds with ideas to change the world. These ideas start off as concepts of a way to do something better, cheaper, and faster that allow a particular market to gain a valuable new product that solves a critical need for customers and for them to be delighted by the new product. The transition from idea to full-fledged product and investing and funding the idea from early stage ideation to later stage scale and growth needs investors. To be an early-stage investor is incredibly high risk because, ultimately, it's utterly uncertain that the startup will succeed towards an exit because investors don't have a valuation of a company, don't have proof of a founding team to be able to execute, or a concrete set of customers buying the developed product. Investors are throwing a dart at an opportunity in the future.

Risk is scary for some people and exhilarating for others and all the in-betweens.

The more an investor is comfortable with risk, the better decisions they will make. Investors will become less afraid to experiment or invest in innovation, which, on multiple levels of technology readiness and market validation, is unknown. Conducting thorough assessments and effectively mitigating both internal and external risks significantly enhances the likelihood of impactful investor journeys.

To catalyze innovation by investing, return on investment should be synonymous with return on impact. The entrepreneurial journey is arduous, volatile, extremely risky, and longer than expected, so purposefully impacting the startup ecosystem allows risk to be mitigated and hope to be lifted during the long haul. Solutions that create a transformative impact on a market exhibit greater sustainability and, ultimately, lead to larger financial returns.

Investing in startups requires a particular mindset and psychological approach. Startups often face uncertainties, setbacks, and unexpected challenges. Investors who fund them face those same roadblocks and celebrations alongside their portfolio companies. Traits like resilience, patience, adaptability, and dealing with failures, albeit important to entrepreneurs, also are necessary for investors to embrace. Investors should engage in strategies for making rational decisions, creating a values-aligned portfolio, managing emotions, and maintaining a long-term perspective. Understanding the psychological aspects of startup investing can help investors navigate the emotional rollercoaster and stay focused on their financial investment goals. A startup investor's influence and impact through dedicated involvement in a market or ecosystem extend far beyond the potential of achieving a rare, large exit. While aiming for a spectacular exit is a common goal in startup investing, like wrangling unicorns, it's essential to recognize that the journey itself is filled with meaningful contributions, legacy generation, and far-reaching impacts.

i. What is a startup?

A startup company refers to a newly established business venture that aims to develop and deliver innovative products or solutions in the marketplace to a targeted customer. The prime characteristic of startups is that the founding team wants to solve a problem, ultimately delighting the customer and influencing a market with a solid and sustainable competitive advantage. Startups are typically distinguished by their potential for rapid growth, scalability, and disruptive business models.

A startup company is characterized by its focus on developing a new product or solution while simultaneously presenting an investable business model that enables potential funders to recognize the opportunity for substantial returns on their investment. Great startups are forged with strong character and unwavering grit by founding teams who possess a profound passion for solving a specific problem and transforming the customer experience. They tirelessly work to disrupt and revolutionize their respective marketplaces. Startups are not exclusively bound to venture-backed paths; however, they often possess deep-rooted technology or a competitive advantage that grants them a critical edge over existing competitors and new entrants.

The outliers to this definition include startups that originate from an idea loosely scribbled on the back of an envelope or a cocktail napkin in a coffee shop in Silicon Valley. Additionally, there are startups led by seasoned serial entrepreneurs who possess a wealth of knowledge and experience, enabling them to execute with precision and seek high valuations due to their extensive network and expertise. These are not the startups that are referenced in this book. The startups showcased in this book exemplify extraordinary resilience, insurmountable passion, and an unwavering drive for market dominance. It is precisely these exceptional qualities that investors are strongly encouraged to be more mindful of investing in such extraordinary startups.

In contrast to traditional businesses, which may concentrate on incremental improvements or established markets, startups frequently endeavor to create something entirely novel or drastically enhance existing offerings. For investors interested in funding a particular startup, the typical sectors tend to be deep tech, software, CPG (Consumer Product Goods), biotechnology, SAAS (Software as a Service), medical devices, diagnostics, and other emerging industries. Startup companies frequently encounter significant challenges as they operate in dynamic environments and pursue ambitious goals with limited resources such as team, talent, and funding. Startup culture is filled with experimentation, risk-taking, courage, determination, passion, tenacity, and adaptability. Startups are inherently driven to secure market share and generate revenue, especially during challenging economic periods like recessions and downturns. In such circumstances, the importance of early traction becomes even more pronounced and amplified because establishing a solid foundation in the market right from the beginning becomes pivotal for ensuring enduring sustainability in the long run. These volatile times are exceptional opportunities for innovators to exploit niches that might go unnoticed by giant corporations, take advantage of new gaps in the market, and leverage changing customer landscapes.

Pivots are not just critical but also pivotal for maintaining ongoing competitive advantage in today's rapidly evolving business landscape. In an ever-changing market, the ability to pivot strategically and effectively can make all the difference between a startup's success and failure. A pivot refers to a significant shift in a startup's business model, product offering, target market, or overall strategy. A pivot allows a company to adapt to new market dynamics, customer preferences, or emerging opportunities when implemented thoughtfully. Embracing pivots as part of an iterative and agile approach to business is vital. Startups must continuously monitor and analyze market feedback, customer behavior, and industry trends to identify potential areas for improvement or expansion. Leapfrogging any challenges based on input from values-aligned investors and expert advisors critically increases the chances of survival in a continual low-sum, challenging startup game.

To support their growth and development, startups often seek external funding from friends and family (after bootstrapping), angel investors, venture capitalists, or through crowdfunding platforms (See Chapter 1, Section ii, for all Startup Funding Stages). These investments fuel research and development, product refinement, marketing efforts, talent acquisition, and expansion into new markets. Having investors with the same growth mindset, giving posture, problem-solving ethos, and financial and business acumen enhances the technical and business rigor of the startup journey.

As startups evolve and achieve strategic milestones, significant traction, and revenue growth, they may eventually transition into more established companies, expand their operations, or even undergo mergers and acquisitions. However, not all startups succeed, and many face significant challenges along their journey due to market dynamics, competition, funding constraints, or other factors. Traditionally, the startup landscape has been known for its challenging and highly competitive nature, with only one out of every ten startups managing to survive and eventually achieve a meaningful exit. Therefore, the vast majority of startups face numerous hurdles and may need assistance to reach their intended goals. However, it's essential to view this statistic not just as a daunting reality but equally as a source of motivation and inspiration. For entrepreneurs and startup founders, it reminds them of the importance of resilience, perseverance, and a growth mindset. Learning from failures and setbacks, iterating on ideas, and continuously seeking ways to improve can significantly increase a startup's chances of continued progress. With determination, adaptability, and a passion for creating value, startups can increase their likelihood of being among the exceptional few that realize their full potential and leave a legacy.

INVEST IN THE CHANGE YOU WANT TO SEE IN THE WORLD

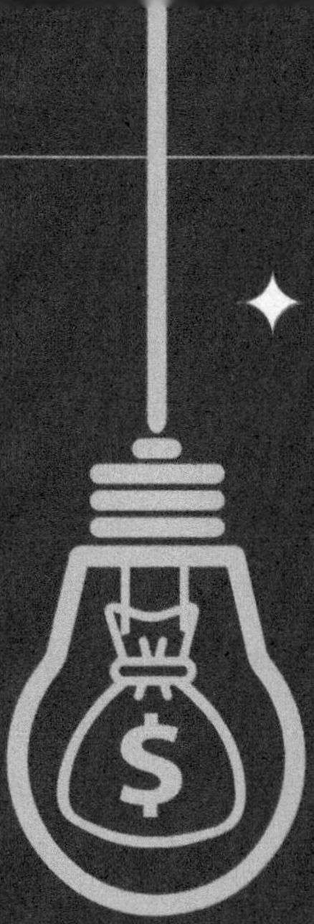

ii. What is a startup investor?

A startup investor invests in a startup to seek potential financial returns and contribute to the venture's scalability plans; belief, hope, business acumen, and influence are all bundled up into trusting that disruptive innovation can go from idea to market. Since they provide capital in the earliest stages of a business and fund the riskiest era of the startup journey, most startup investors invest in the change they want to see in the world. For this guide, the definition of a startup investor is an early-stage angel investor or early-stage venture capitalist that invests in companies at the pre-seed to seed stage. Their primary role and responsibility are to provide the 3 C's of capital, meaning access to **financial capital**, their own and others with possible sustainable or ongoing follow-on investment, access to **network capital,** connections with purpose and warm introductions, and access to **expertise capital**, strategic, technical or business support for streamlined startup growth. (See Figure 2 – What is a Startup Investor?)

Investor profiles exhibit a wide range of diversity, stemming from each investor's distinctive lived experiences, curated careers, deep expertise, leadership qualities, and preferences regarding investment opportunities and choices. Startup investors are not friends and family of the founder or the founding team. They are not biased in selecting the startup to invest in based on their familial or personal relationships. Startup investors fund potentially successful startups based on their business acumen, expertise, and decision-making around all five M's of investing (See Chapter 6).

What is a startup investor?

An early-stage investor is an individual who invests a part of her personal wealth in a company that is usually in its start-up phase. She makes her competence, experience and network of contacts available to the entrepreneur.

What really is a startup investor?

Early-stage investing is a partnership between the investor and a startup company & its team. After the investment, their financial successes become aligned.
If the startup is successful, then the investor shares in that success.

Provides 3C's of Capital:

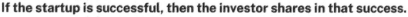

NETWORK CAPITAL	EXPERTISE CAPITAL	FINANCIAL CAPITAL
• Connections of Purpose • Warm Introductions	• Strategic & Advisory expertise • Technical prowess	• Wire or Checks • Sustainable & Ongong

© She Invest'd 2023

Figure 2

Understanding the stages of startup funding and the corresponding investor types is invaluable for investors seeking to gain a clear understanding of the specific phase they are investing in. This knowledge enables them to plan more effectively for future funding rounds and make informed decisions that align with the startup's growth trajectory. The essential early-stage startup stages are: (See Figure 3 – The Startup Funding Stages)

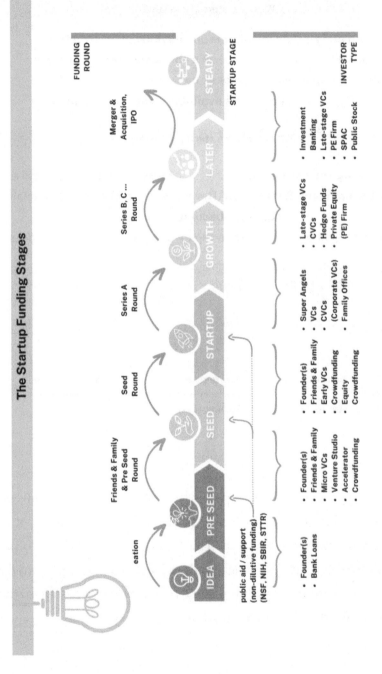

Figure 3

1. Idea Stage

- ⊙ Idea to MVP (minimal viable product)
- ⊙ An idea-stage startup represents a nascent venture in the earliest phase, where the focus lies primarily on conceptualizing, refining, and validating the business idea, often with limited tangible progress or established product development.
- ⊙ Founder and Founding Team Bootstrap Funding

2. Seed Stage

- ⊙ Proof of concept phase (some are to market), Pre-seed, and Seed Stages
- ⊙ During the initial phase of development, seed stage startups commonly seek funding to validate their business idea, conduct market research, and construct an MVP (Minimum Viable Product).
- ⊙ Funding from: Friends and Family, Angel Investor, Grant Funding

3. Startup Stage

- ⊙ Early-stage / Product Development, first institutional round / Series A (early sales and manufacturing funds)
- ⊙ A startup stage company that has a primary focus on securing funding to facilitate rapid expansion, generating recurring revenue, and achieving substantial market traction.
- ⊙ Funding from: Super Angels, VC (Venture Capital), CVC (Corporate Venture Capital) Funding

4. Growth Stage

- ⊙ Varies depending on industry, including these stages:
  - Second round / Series B (Working capital, not turning profit)

- Third round / Series B or C (Expansion, turning profit)
- Fourth round (Finance the "going public" phase)

⊙ A growth-stage startup is a company that has successfully established its product in the market, demonstrating consistent revenue growth, expanding its customer base, and focusing on scaling operations to capture a larger market share.

⊙ Funding from: Family Office, VC, CVC Funding

5. Later Stage

⊙ IPO (Initial Public Offering) or acquisition (sale of the entire company, acquihire, etc.) to another (typically larger) company

⊙ A late-stage startup refers to a company that has progressed beyond the initial growth and development phases, typically with an established product or service, significant market presence, and a focus on scaling operations, expanding into new markets, and preparing for potential exit opportunities such as an IPO or acquisition.

⊙ Funding from: Investment Bank, CVC, PE (Private Equity), SPAC (Special Purpose Acquisition Company)

6. Steady Stage

⊙ The steady-state stage for startups denotes a phase characterized by relative stability and balance.

⊙ During this period, the company has demonstrated a sustainable business model, reliable revenue streams, and operational efficiency. The primary emphasis at this stage lies in scaling and optimizing existing operations rather than pursuing rapid growth or significant pivots.

Awareness of where an investor funds startups along this continuum is critical in assessing early-stage valuations, time to market, and product-market fit. Many investors are curious about crowdfunding and equity crowdfunding, so I will dive in quickly to clarify. I have invested in many Kickstarter campaigns and products, including The Sash Bag and Tiger Friday. I have also enjoyed prospecting equity crowdfunding campaigns on my platform of choice, Wefunder (exemplified by Nostalgia Coffee Roasters, Babe Kambucha, and Lil' Libros), and exploring opportunities and challenges with colleagues like Equity Crowdfunding Week leaders. Crowdfunding platforms allow funders (or backers) to fund opportunities with a finite reward post-investment, like a product, bundle of products, experiences, or, if they are a software company, a code for beta testing their technology. Platforms like Kickstarter or Indiegogo provide this very low-risk solution to get innovative new products into the hands of investors and customers alike. Anyone can essentially help a new company jump-start its journey by pre-purchasing a product or solution or for established companies to fund a brand-new product launch. It's exhilarating when, as a backer, you get a brand-new product in your hands. Backers are not buying a piece of the company, investing in the team, or the startup's growth opportunity.

However, there are two main reasons crowdfunding supports startup success regarding the startup investor mindset:

1. **Customer validation.** This early form of customer discovery and buyer behavior is beneficial for more accurately projecting revenue. Being involved as a customer in this process, the future investor can gain concrete and actual insight into the customer buying journey and be part of the community of early adopters to gain further insight into behaviors, feedback, and customer service.

2. **Testing operations efficiency.** An excellent approach to evaluating the operational efficiencies of manufacturing, distribution, and shipping of products is to put the plan into action and execute it. Through a crowdfunding campaign, entrepreneurs can test the accuracy, dependencies, and timing of the entire operations from production to last-mile delivery and customer service. Investor's risk decreases in the early stages just by this process being tested with customers to allow for actual quality control and learnings from the entire supply chain process.

Equity crowdfunding platforms like Wefunder, Republic, and StartEngine enable investors to fund startups at a very low dollar amount, typically starting at as little as $100. It's also a way to get acquainted with the type of companies that seek funding from investors, review pitch decks, evaluate teams' bios, investigate what a lead investor communicates about a startup, and examine who backs these early-stage companies. The campaigns are typically public, and an investor can scroll through the platform to explore. This type of investment values the crowd to fill a fundraising round for a startup from accredited and non-accredited investors. Let's just stop here to define accredited and non-accredited investors. There are ~14 different ways to characterize an accredited investor through the SEC (Securities and Exchange Commission). Most commonly (and most aligned to the investors reading this guide), accredited investors are individuals who earn over a certain amount of money (in 2023, for a single individual is $200,000 or spousal equivalent over of $300,000) or have a net worth over a certain threshold (in 2023 an individual or spousal equivalent of at least $1 million, not including the value of their primary residence). It constantly changes, so a quick look at the SEC website will allow the most current qualifications (www.sec.gov). This designation or rule helps mitigate risk, proving that the investors have a certain amount of sophistication to invest in a precarious asset class and have the financial cushion to weather this type of lengthy and uncertain investment opportunity.

The next tier of investor type is the angel investors, typically accredited investors, wealthy individuals, who provide early-stage funding to startups in exchange for equity or ownership in the company. They often play a crucial role in bridging the funding gap that exists between friends and family and institutional investors. This allocation typically includes investments into startups in the pre-seed and seed stages (MVP to the first customer, depending on the industry). This type of investment can be accomplished as an individual investor, angel group, angel network, syndication network, or platforms like AngelList. The final tier in early-stage investments is the VC phase. Investors can participate in the venture capitalist round in a couple of different roles: GP (General Partner), MP (Managing Partner), LP (Limited Partner), IC (Investment Committee - who are typically either GPs, MPs, or LPs), venture scout, startup mentor, venture analyst, and business advisor. This list of opportunities provides a broad overview of the entire venture capital (VC) landscape and the potential areas where early-stage investors can actively participate. There are variations as diverse and unique as the hues of a rainbow of every stage of the early-stage investment landscape (angel investors can be VCs, lead an angel group, dabble in equity crowdfunding or not, and/or join syndication networks that all have different rules of entry). I intentionally use the more descriptive term "hues" to emphasize the vast array of variations instead of the phrase "colors of the rainbow" as it implies a limited and finite set of traditional colors. Diversity among investors is limitless and boundless.

I NTEGRITY-DRIVEN

N ETWORKED

V ALUABLE

E NGAGED

S INCERE

T RUSTWORTHY

O PEN-MINDED

R ISK-TOLERATING

The mindset of an early-stage investor needs to be expansive, open-minded, and adaptable to opportunities and volatility. That is certainly difficult when starting out because most people want to obtain a set instructional manual of how, why, where, and whom to invest in. Only proposed guardrails exist to continue an impactful journey, and early-stage investors need to be as comfortable as possible in navigating the ambiguity. A startup investor embraces being "I"ntegrity-driven, "N"etworked, "V"aluable, "E"ngaged, "S"incere, "T"rustworthy, "O"pen-minded, and "R"isk-tolerating.

Startup investors fund companies with the aspiration of capturing the vibrant spectrum of potential financial returns while playing a part in the kaleidoscope of the venture's ongoing milestone achievements and entrepreneurial journey. Investing in various distinct phases of a startup's journey and at different stages of venture funding, from product-focused to close-to-exit, is akin to savoring the vibrant spectrum of opportunities, each presenting its unique hue within the rainbow of entrepreneurial potential.

iii. Connecting to a Thriving Startup Ecosystem

The living, breathing, dynamic startup ecosystem is the most fantastic community to be included in, welcomed, invest time and treasure in, and impact. I have been a devotee and a passionate activist in this network for over a decade as an investor, advocate, educator, entrepreneur, and catalyst; I would do the journey (even with all of its failures, learnings, and challenges) all over again. The investor who wants to profoundly impact and influence this active community should engage in it actively, frequently, and with intentionality and conviction. Why do I say these things? The investor who is not entirely involved in a community does not have or feel the pulse of the ecosystem. To experience the pulse, an investor must be committed. Investors should actively support entrepreneurs to the extent that they can genuinely empathize with their perspective and challenges, enough so to feel what it's like to walk a mile along their journey and in their unique boots. Roll up the sleeves of strategy with entrepreneurs. Connect with all stakeholders of a thriving community. Investors should examine the startup industry carefully and consciously, including key players, trends, and dynamics; then understand the value chain in the startup ecosystem and the valuable, impactful place they make as individuals. Map it out. Know it, engage in it, invest in it.

A thriving community depends on passionate investors, entrepreneurs, connectors, builders, service providers, banks, and lawyers, who care enough about the broader economic impact of a geography or industry to tend the community in organic ways like pitch competitions, events that promote innovation and meetups to gain relational knowledge, amongst many others. It's a jigsaw puzzle of diverse pieces and sizes to build a diverse community, be that valuable piece that stakeholders seek and can be plugged in when needed. This startup ecosystem can be distilled into five sections (See Figure 4 - The Dynamic Ecosystem Startup Ecosystem Stakeholders):

The Dynamic Startup Ecosystem Stakeholders

Entrepreneurs
- Solo entrepreneurs
- Tech founders and co-Founders
- Founding Teams

Investors
- Individuals
- Groups
- Networks
- Funds

Talent
- Universities
- Trade Orgs
- Professional Orgs
- Affinity Groups

INNOVATION

Resources
- Mentors
- Advisors
- Lawyers
- Accountants
- CFOs/CTOs/CSOs

Support
- Accelerators
- Incubators
- Coworking Spaces
- Economic Dev Orgs
- Industry Orgs

© She Invests! 2023

Figure 4

1. **Entrepreneurs.** At the core of the innovation economy, entrepreneurs are individuals who embody the spirit of innovation, creativity, and resourcefulness, who create ideas and launch ventures. They possess a strong drive to identify and pursue opportunities, take calculated risks, and are passionate, resilient, and relentless in their pursuit of turning their visions into reality. Founders are the innovators, the mavericks, and the trailblazers.

2. **Investors.** When embracing a purposeful startup investor mindset, investors can provide financial capital as well as fundamental support for the launch and scale of exceptional founders and transformational startups. Investors can be individual funders, groups of investors, syndication networks, or funds, influencing the ongoing success of the entire ecosystem in various ways. Investors are the connected catalysts, the risk-takers, and the enthusiasts.

3. **Talent.** During the startup journey, various sets of talented team members are required. It starts with developers at the earliest stages, tasked with creating a working prototype, and later on, marketing support becomes essential to achieve growth stage market dominance. Hubs of talent for all aspects of a growing startup can be universities, technology hubs, trade organizations, professional organizations, and affinity groups (groups of a specific industry or sub-industry like coding groups, social media marketing groups, etc.). Talent teams are the efficient executors, the bold builders, and the engines.

4. **Support.** The startup journey is very lonely and unknown, so support organizations and individuals who assist in the economic development of the innovation ecosystem, typically their core personal mission, play a pivotal role in connecting startups and all stakeholders within the community. They are the glue, serving as the constellation-builders of shiny bright ideas and humans. Included in this group are accelerators, incubators, coworking spaces, economic development organizations, and industry-specific conglomerates. The support teams are the architects, the caregivers, and the believers.

5. **Resources.** Essential resources for the ongoing launch and growth
   of startup ventures can bring targeted support and provide trusted
   and vetted introductions to entrepreneurs. Resources include (but
   are not limited to) mentors, advisors, lawyers, accountants,
   CFOs/CTOs/CSOs (Chief Financial Officers/Chief Technical
   Officers/Chief Strategy or Scientific Officers), etc. Most resources
   provide targeted expertise and guidance to navigate complex startup
   growth frameworks and mitigate most risks, enabling startups to
   focus on their core business activities with confidence. The resources
   team are the boundary pushers, the builders, and the collaborators.

When investors engage with all of these players (individuals or groups), this allows investors to truly understand and appreciate who can help that entrepreneur along the startup journey (and equally with a funder's own startup journey). Investors, albeit aspiring investors or experienced investors, I encourage you to map the ecosystem that supports the growth of an industry. Mapping the startup economy in the investor's zone of influence (local, national, or international and of varying volumes) is a great way to get familiar and seek more introductions and connections. The StartupCinci resource map is one of my favorites. Know the groups and individuals, the influential leaders, and the networkers; write their names down and connect with them on LinkedIn. Investors should know that their investment (or check/wire) positively affects a startup's stability and is extremely important to a founder. Still, the capital, surrounded by resources and support from various vetted and trusted resources that an investor has purposefully built around themselves, makes all the difference in the world and allows that entrepreneur to truly soar and scale.

Engaging in an investor's ecosystem can be daunting at times. The concerted effort will pay off. Connecting with valuable stakeholders can take a couple of routes: meeting over coffee and conversations (with both entrepreneurs and other investors), attending events, participating as a mentor, assisting as a judge, volunteering with economic development organizations like the SBDC (Small Business Development Center) or organizations like Stella Foundation. These actions allow investors to get plugged in, interact, meet, and get acquainted with the players in the field. Undeniably, these types of activities also significantly increase and broaden deal flow. It's not a waste of time. This way of staying attuned to the startup community will also assist an investor in funding the best deals. An investor might be having an investor meeting with a founder who is pitching for funding, and that investor has seen the entrepreneur two or three times within the ecosystem at a pitch competition or a networking event. These connection points increase familiarity and trust and decrease risk. That investor can assume that the founder is more likely to have support from the accelerator leading the pitch competition or the professional organization putting on the networking event. By being involved in multiple events and opportunities, entrepreneurs are signaling that they are receptive to seeking resources and are open to being advised to improve their business offering or path to market. Investors can then contact startup advocates during the due diligence phase of inquiry to gain more insight, ultimately de-risking the investment. Thus, funding becomes more informed and conscious. If an investor has never seen a founder at any community get-together, has not evaluated them as a judge at a pitch event, and has not seen them being active with support organizations, that sends a red flag of how the startup is effectively launching and growing, as well as being coachable. The assumption then becomes that the startup founder(s) are working so much in their business that they are not interacting with others as much as they should to gain mentorship, share resources with other entrepreneurs, and receive valuable feedback. This de-risking of investment opportunities through community, collaboration, and connectivity is vital for achieving external and community validation and insight into the startup business model, traction, and leadership team.

This entire web of considerations ensures the ongoing sustainability of a longer-term thriving startup investor portfolio. Engaging in the ecosystem as an investor can also increase influence amongst investors and entrepreneurs, thus making co-investments, syndication, and deal sharing more manageable and collaborative, again decreasing risk.

Lastly, investors can create a hub and spoke map of the great influencers in their network; this helps them stay focused and intentionally build a trusted community. There might be specific organizations or individuals with excellent presence or leadership in the startup community whom investors should more actively engage with. Being focused on intentional connections makes for a healthier pre- and post-investment journey. Embracing a mindset of connected webs of influence and picturing a hub and spoke model of a startup ecosystem is a supreme way of multiplying impact as an investor. An investment goes beyond a mere "check"; it encompasses the resources and networks linked to that check, enabling the startup to flourish.

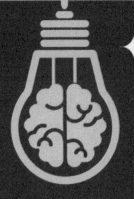

MINDSET

OVER

MONEY

Chapter 2

Embracing the Investor Mindset

Agreat, impactful, and thoughtful investor typically is the most supportive, dedicated, insightful, and mindful investor, especially in the early-stage investment world. Investors assess a startup's potential for growth while optimistically providing capital to a founding team with uncertain future financial returns. This takes an abundance growth mindset, fully understanding the risks involved yet being proactive in providing support to a founding team with sufficient passion to withstand the storms of the startup journey. Investors need to consider factors such as customer acquisition, market validation, revenue generation, potential partnerships, intellectual property, and any existing prototypes or minimum viable products. Evidence of early traction and validation provides confidence to investors regarding the startup's potential. This type of investor, the great ones, are typically also the most respected, sought after, and impactful because they build relationships and increase trust between and amongst investors and entrepreneurs alike. Investors can purposefully grow to be great. It takes intentionality (reading this book) and focus for the greater startup good.

The investor mindset that fosters economic growth and facilitates the successful journey of innovations from inception to market and eventual scaling and exit embodies nine key attributes. These key considerations are organized in a matrix, which allows for a comprehensive analysis of an investor's overall posture, keeping the north star of empathy at the center.

To utilize the matrix effectively, investors can engage in journaling about each characteristic, reflecting on how they manifest in their investment approach. This introspective exercise helps raise awareness of strengths and areas that may require improvement. By purposefully taking action to enhance the identified aspects, investors can cultivate a more well-rounded and practical approach to supporting startups.

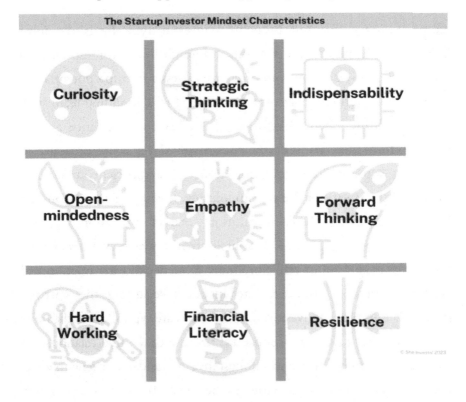

Figure 5

To define and elaborate on these core nine characteristics:

1. **Curiosity.** Curiosity drives investors to continuously seek the most inspirational innovations that will make the most significant impact and seek new knowledge and insights for themselves. It involves asking thought-provoking questions, staying curious about emerging technologies, and actively seeking to understand the nuances of the industries they invest in. According to Hogue, curiosity drives creativity, a true symbiotic relationship. Without curiosity, creativity does not exist. In a magical transfer, curiosity leads to creativity which leads to innovation. This is why investors who are curious are drawn to products and startups created by spectacular founders who fearlessly innovate.

2. **Strategic Thinking.** Making informed decisions in a sea of adversity and uncertainty through strategic thinking allows investors to see the big picture and be able to score or vet opportunities appropriately. It involves analyzing market dynamics, identifying trends, and assessing competitive landscapes, thus providing entrepreneurs with guidance on market positioning, business models, and growth strategies.

3. **Indispensability.** There are many talented founders, engineers, and innovators creating the next big breakthrough product. Investing in the best opportunities often involves a certain level of competition, as these opportunities typically represent highly investable and promising startups. These founders will need to find the best investors who will be partners through the journey of an early-stage company. Founders do their own due diligence for the right values-aligned investors. Investors who make themselves indispensable through constructive feedback, excellent advising,

meaningful mentoring, and an abundance mindset approach to network introductions are highly coveted by the best innovative startups.

4. **Open-mindedness.** Embracing various perspectives and ideas, sourcing diverse startups, and reaching deeper and broader into networks creates an open-minded, inclusive process and, ultimately, the growth of investor portfolios for increased return on investment. Investors can identify opportunities that others may overlook by being receptive to different approaches, market insights, and business solutions. This mindset encourages the exploration of unconventional ideas in underestimated markets, leading to breakthrough innovations and market disruption.

5. **Empathy.** Empathy is the heart of the investor mindset. Empathy allows investors to understand and connect with the experiences, challenges, and emotions of the entrepreneurs and founding teams they fund and the customers being served by their purposeful products. When investors place themselves in the founders' shoes, they can offer more valuable guidance, support, and constructive feedback to the startup team. Empathy helps foster a stronger investor-entrepreneur relationship, leading to better collaboration and mutual trust.

6. **Forward Thinking.** Early-stage investing is the business of investing in the future of what most cannot envision, and many miss as an opportunity. Will there be robots in every home? Will there be flying cars? Will new food sources from artificial intelligence solve global food shortages? We cannot predict the future. However, by conducting research on trends, emerging markets, new research areas and imagining through strategic thought, investors can start to create

their own predictions of where markets might be in 10 or 20 years. This process informs their investment thesis and decisions. The more forward-thinking and clearer an investor is of the possible future, the easier it will be to source and pick the startup winners.

7. **Hard Working.** Most early-stage investors conduct rigorous research, keeping their ears to the ground through proactive networking and communicating with startup advocates, accelerators, universities, and other investment groups. They typically do this on the weekends, nights, before work, and in their "free time." They are hard at work distilling the research, networks, trends, meetings, analysis, connections, and pitches that are the tactical elements of the funding continuum of sourcing, evaluating, investing, and supporting startups.

8. **Financial Literacy.** Introducing the not-so-glamorous side of investing: finance, accounting, and projections. The investor's world is grounded in sound financial acumen. A money mindset of knowledge and growth makes investors strong supporters of great startups. Investors should possess a solid understanding of financial analysis, burn rates, cap tables, valuation methods, supply chain issues impacting the bottom line, financial modeling, and investment frameworks. Great investors don't gamble; they take calculated risks. Investors are trying to project what kind of revenue or profitability a company can generate in the future, typically when there is just a model and signals towards possible early revenue. A note to those feeling overwhelmed by this characteristic; don't worry, it can be taught or advised. Investors typically have a strong network of financial gurus who can help with deeper analysis for an informed investment decision. If an investor's network is in its infancy, reach out to organizations that support entrepreneurs and investors to find

their best financial contacts to continue sourcing those who align with values, character, and industry. However, most investors should have a solid level of financial literacy through their own experience, education, and lifelong learning. You will get there!

9. **Resilience.** As previously emphasized, early-stage investing represents one of the riskiest asset classes. When combined with the startup economy's inherent volatility and unpredictable nature, a startup investor must demonstrate resilience. Startups often face challenges, setbacks, and pivots along their journey. By maintaining unwavering dedication as an investor while advocating and supporting entrepreneurs in their startup journey, founders are encouraged to persevere in the challenging startup environment, surmount obstacles, and ultimately achieve growth amidst challenges.

Why is this posture important? If you're talking about return on investment, undoubtedly, investors will be presented with the best deal flow because funders want to invest with other like-minded, trustworthy investors. Trust must be highly coveted and prioritized, regarded as invaluable and highly esteemed. The value chain of a single investor stems from these qualities and is multiplied as that investor gives more than they receive. As an investor continues through their own startup funding journey, with every decision made, that investor is creating a more insightful investment thesis and decision-making matrix that will allow the next entrepreneur to be evaluated better and, ultimately, be better served.

i. Assessing Risk Appetite, Conducting Risk Assessment, and Implementing Risk Management Strategies.

Investing in early-stage startups offers a potential for high rewards but also carries significant risks, emphasizing the need to strike a delicate balance between risk and reward. To minimize risk, investors should understand their own risk appetite, assess the risk of every investment being funded, manage risk by diversifying portfolios (by many parameters like industry, number, product type, and stage), research through due diligence the business potential of every investment, and the list goes on. Risk appetite refers to an investor's willingness and capacity to tolerate risk based on their individual and financial goals, backgrounds, investment strategies, investing knowledge, financial situations, and personal preferences. The risk spectrum ranges from investors with a higher risk appetite, who embrace the challenge of funding startups with greater uncertainty, to those with a lower risk appetite, who adopt a more conservative and cautious approach when investing in startups. Understanding and defining risk appetite helps investors align their investment decisions with their desired level of risk exposure. Initiating this process involves documenting a funder's financial goals in relation to early-stage startup investing, reflecting on the individual risk perception through journaling, and establishing a range of risk appetite —low, medium, or high— that aligns with an appropriate comfort level. Engaging in the practice of writing down money mindset thoughts and discussing them with fellow investors for self-evaluation and self-reflection can yield significant benefits. To embark on this journaling journey, look to the end of this section for helpful prompts. Taking that first step to put pen to paper allows investors to gain a deeper understanding of their constraints and opportunities, ultimately leading to better self-awareness and embracing their unique perspectives.

Having established their internal barometer of risk, investors can now shift their focus to examining the foundation and projections of the startup. The next consideration is assessing the risk of a potential investment. For early-stage investors, assessing the risk of a potential investment includes evaluating market dynamics, competitive landscape, team capabilities, technology risks, scalability challenges, regulatory and legal factors, and financial viability. Investors assess each of these risks to evaluate the probability and potential impact on the overall investment, enabling them to effectively manage their risk exposure.

Mitigating and managing risks effectively can be accomplished by increasing diversification, conducting rigorous due diligence, and being actively involved in the startup's growth. Diversification plays a critical role in risk mitigation as it spreads risk across multiple investments, reducing the impact of any individual startup's failure. This aspect carries immense importance, especially considering that only a select few ideas evolve into actual startups, and most startups in a portfolio may achieve sustained viability. Thorough due diligence allows investors to identify and assess specific risks by diving into market research, conducting customer interviews, checking on industry comparables, validating (as much as an investor can at the early stage) the exit potential, and assessing the strength of the founding team to weather the uncertainty of early-stage startup growth. Active involvement in their investments allows investors to closely monitor progress, support the startup's strategy for growth, identify and address emerging risks, and make timely adjustments to mitigate risks. Taking an additional step beyond an individual's due diligence, engaging in this type of review with a group of angels is often highly advantageous, typically yielding significant benefits and added value. The Angel Capital Association (ACA) serves as an excellent resource for discovering exceptional angel groups with a wide range of specializations, such as geographic focus, industry-specific expertise, gender-specific interests, and impact-driven initiatives tailored to specific stages of investment. Most of these angel groups place great emphasis on thorough due diligence. Being affiliated with this prestigious organization, individual angels and group leaders highly value ongoing education, as well as gaining knowledge through participation in panels, workshops, and summits. Researching and discussing risks and mitigations in an investment group's due diligence meetings and, ultimately, Due Diligence Report (or Investment Memo) provides transparency to all investors. This formulaic process ensures that all investors are fully informed about the risks associated with the investment opportunity, which can help prevent misunderstandings and assist in managing the investment over time for optimal return on investment and return on impact.

The risk assessment and management cycle is never static. Risk management is an ongoing process that extends beyond the initial investment decision and way beyond the check (or wire). Early-stage investors continuously monitor the risks associated with their investments throughout the startup's journey. They stay updated on market trends, regulatory changes, startup valuation updates, and other external factors that could impact the investment. By actively monitoring and managing risks, investors can evaluate and respond to emerging challenges, identify evolving internal and external risk landscapes, pivot when necessary, and take proactive steps to protect and enhance the value and success of their investments.

It's easy to paint a negative picture of all of the risks of a startup. As a startup investor, embrace the challenge of assessing how the company, team, and advisors effectively mitigate, manage, and reduce risks. Risks are real, for sure, and by conducting a rigorous risk assessment to identify and assess risks associated with a potential investment opportunity, investors can make informed decisions about the level of risk they are willing to take on. Then, in the endless circle of life-long learning and evaluation, investors can re-assess their risk appetite —low, medium, or high— and make adjustments if necessary.

Life experiences significantly contribute to an investor's risk tolerance and management capabilities. Diving into this personal piece of risk is delicate but essential. Investors' risk tolerance significantly shapes their career trajectory, personal financial journey, life path, and the intergenerational influences they inherit. As an investor, it is crucial to be fully aware of your risk tolerance level and approach investment decisions with open eyes. Investors need to be mindful of the strengths in their money story, meaning that they might know how to budget effectively, read financial projections, or grow revenue as an entrepreneur. Investors can truly thrive and find inner peace while seeking comfort in these strengths. It's not only about monetary wealth but owning a broader mindset encompassing various dimensions of life and overall prosperity and fulfillment.

Investors should also be aware of their shadows and acknowledge their gaps. Shadows can manifest as deep-seated fears around money, rooted in childhood experiences of scarcity or anxieties about potential financial losses. Gaps, on the other hand, represent areas of unfamiliarity or limited awareness. To foster personal and financial growth, investors can embrace a growth mindset and actively seek to acquire the knowledge and insights to fill those gaps. When startups encounter challenges such as lack of profitability, suboptimal outcomes, difficulties in fundraising, or eventual closure, shadows, and gaps begin to emerge in their journey.

Now, let's delve into the rewarding aspect of being a startup investor. The reward is that you can make a considerable multiple (the definition of "considerable multiple" is debated depending on the time horizon, industry, and thesis, so it can go from 5x to 70x). Investors can also not make money at all with dead startups, make their money back, or a small multiple. Considering the statistics that only 1 in 10 startups succeed, it becomes crucial to do the math and recognize that the one or two surviving investments have the potential to compensate for the total of approximately two dozen investments made. Understanding this potential upside is essential in managing expectations and making informed investment decisions.

Let's embark on a comprehensive exploration of economic empowerment, with a particular focus on the impact investing sphere and the realm of the women's startup economy (from women-led startups gaining support to women-specific products finally coming to market). Through delving into this discourse, investors can gain profound insights, exploring the transformative potential of impact investing in reshaping startup success metrics. The driving hypothesis at the core of startup support initiatives posits that by offering increased assistance, mentoring, and effective advisory services, coupled with the cultivation of more robust and more aligned networks, facilitation of warm introductions, and the establishment of robust startup resource pipelines, a higher number of startups can navigate the challenging early stages and thrive. This comprehensive approach aims to empower startups by equipping them with the necessary tools and guidance to overcome obstacles and achieve sustainability.

Investors who are deeply committed to fostering the growth of startups firmly believe in the potential to achieve a more balanced ratio of success and failure. They envision a future where the survival rate of startups reaches a promising 50-50, meaning an equal proportion of startups succeed and progress to become thriving businesses.

Moreover, some of the most optimistic investors go even further and propose a collective effort to fill the gap, ensuring the survival of a remarkable 9 out of 10 startups. They emphasize the importance of meticulous sourcing and evaluation of the best mix of startup founding teams, innovative solutions, and target markets. By conducting rigorous due diligence and strategically aligning investments with startups that demonstrate the most promising potential, these visionary investors aim to maximize the chances of success for a vast majority of startups. Highlighting the significance of nurturing a conducive environment for startups, this vision challenges the traditional view of startup failure. It underscores the importance of proactive support and thoughtful investment strategies that align with the startups' unique needs and aspirations.

However, markets are volatile and customers are fickle, global pandemics obliterate supply chains and manufacturers are not consistent in QC (quality control), so most startup entrepreneurs and startup investors cannot foresee the incredible spikes and valleys of an economy. Hence, the true essence of a startup investor mindset lies in the rewarding endeavors of consistent mentoring, impactful influence, and unwavering belief in entrepreneurs and communities. It transcends mere transactions; it fosters relational connections, mutual respect, and significant impact.

Money Mindset Journal

How was money discussed around my dinner table growing up?

....

....

....

....

....

....

....

When I started making money on my own, how did that make me feel?

....

....

....

....

....

....

....

When I had enough money to save, what did I do with it?

....

....

....

....

....

....

....

What type of businesses I know seem like a "great bet," and which are not?

....
....
....
....
....
....

What is your comfort level with investing $100 into an early-stage startup?

....
....
....
....
....
....

What type of startup would you be willing to invest in, why?

....
....
....
....
....
....

What risks have I taken that I was OK with, and which ones was I not?

....
....
....
....
....

What would I like my money mindset to be?

....

....

....

....

....

....

If I was gifted a $50M fund, what would I invest in?

....

....

....

....

....

....

How do I perceive money? Is it something to worry about or not?

....

....

....

....

....

....

ii. Catalyzing Innovation Through Capitalization

Early-stage investors are attracted to startups that offer innovative ideas, disruptive technologies, or unique business models. They seek out ventures that have the potential to revolutionize industries, introduce new products, or address significant market gaps. "Catalyzing innovation through capitalization" refers to the process of fueling and accelerating the pace of innovation by providing the necessary financial resources to support the development and growth of innovative ideas, technologies, or businesses.

Investors are champions and catalyzers. Innovation remains simply a creative idea or research bench lab experiment until it undergoes the catalyzing power of capitalization. By investing in research and development, talent acquisition, technology infrastructure, and strategic marketing, businesses can transform innovative concepts into tangible launches and sustain their growth trajectory. Investors who actively cultivate their mindsets, encompassing both imaginative breadth and depth, can wholeheartedly embrace the high growth potential of early-stage startups. Investors can effectively address a startup's projected market gaps and needs by exploring its potential competitive advantages, even if they are not fully actualized during the initial funding stages. Skillfully identifying signals within scalable markets allows investors to recognize the opportunities for growth and innovation that the startup envisions. The capital infusion of seed funding will enable entrepreneurs to conduct experiments, perform testing, iterate on product designs, develop prototypes, build a minimum viable product (MVP), explore new technologies, and validate their business concepts. Seed funding catalyzes the transformation of ideas into tangible products or solutions by providing the necessary, yet scarce, initial financial resources.

CATALYZE

INNOVATION

BY

INVESTING

Investors who embrace a broad understanding of startups, recognizing their high growth potential while acknowledging their early-stage status, are better positioned to make informed investment decisions. These investors identify and support the untapped disruptive potential within startups. Through crucial funding, meaningful mentorship, and vetted networks, this early-stage advantage accelerates the growth of startups. It maximizes the startups' innovative potential, often introducing disruptive solutions with significant prospects for critical growth and market expansion. Fueling research and development (R & D), investors enable startups to push the boundaries of knowledge, develop breakthrough solutions, and continuously improve their products. By investing in such companies, investors aim to capitalize on the transformative power of these innovations and the progressive influence of these innovators. They seek ventures that challenge established players, disrupt traditional industries, and capture a substantial market share. The ability to achieve rapid and sustainable growth is a primary driver of potential returns on investment for early-stage investors.

Startups that bring innovation and disruption to their respective industries often create a competitive advantage, or moat, especially if the founder has exceptional founder-market fit to differentiate themselves from incumbents and potential market players (See Chapter 6, Section iv, for more insight). Founder-market fit refers to a scenario where the founder(s) possess profound and extensive experience, understanding, or research within the market they are targeting (See FAQ (Frequently Asked Questions) Section for key insights). This advantage empowers founders to build purposeful products that effectively address genuine customer pain points, meeting the precise needs of their target audience. This competitive edge of disruptive innovations that often target large and growing markets can lead to higher market demand, increased customer loyalty, increased possibility of capturing a significant market share, and more prominent barriers to entry for new entrants. Investors acknowledge the significance of investing in startups with distinctive and sustainable competitive advantages, as these ventures are more inclined to experience swift adoption of their innovative solutions and achieve long-term financial viability. These considerations, in turn, enhance the probability of subsequent funding rounds or substantial exits.

Innovation and disruption are often born from identifying unmet market needs or gaps. Startups that can effectively address these gaps by offering innovative solutions have the potential to attract a large customer base. Investors understand that investing in startups with a deep understanding of market dynamics and customer pain points can lead to significant market opportunities. By backing startups that have a strong product-market fit, investors position themselves to benefit from the market demand generated by these innovative solutions.

In addition to addressing the internal needs of a startup, catalyzing innovation through capitalization also fosters the formation of strategic partnerships. Capitalization can enable startups to pursue strategic collaborations or acquire other companies to provide access to complementary technologies, intellectual property, customer bases, distribution channels, or industry expertise. Through capital infusion, investors facilitate innovation by enabling collaboration, consolidation, or the integration of new capabilities within these initiatives.

In nurturing an innovation ecosystem, capitalizing multiple startups attracts exceptional entrepreneurs to choose a desired community, engages and retains top talent, and encourages research institutions to collaborate with stakeholders, all contributing to economic growth. Investors who engage in the innovation culture and actively contribute to establishing and continuously evolving an entire network help foster entrepreneurial activity. These dynamics expedite resource and expertise exchange, encourage collaboration, promote knowledge sharing, and nurture the cross-pollination of ideas to ignite disruptive innovations going to market.

iii. Cultivating a Growth Mindset and Adaptability

Adopting a growth mindset as a startup investor, along with embracing adaptability in mind and mentoring, allows for malleability to help withstand the evolution and uncertainty of the startup's personal journey and collective economy. A growth mindset embodies the belief that individual abilities, intelligence, and talents are not fixed traits but can be nurtured, cultivated, and enhanced through dedication, hard work, effort, resilience, perseverance, and a commitment to lifelong learning. It is a mindset that embraces challenges, sees failures as opportunities for growth, and views effort as a path to mastery. This is especially true for investors. Embracing a growth mindset is crucial for investors, both in their personal journey within the startup world and in their interactions with entrepreneurs. It influences their approach as they mentor founders, make investment decisions, evaluate and select numerous startups, and foster participatory growth within investor networks and innovation ecosystems. Believing in others and supporting growth is how to stay positive and optimistic in this high-risk asset class.

The notion of a growth mindset gained prominence through psychologist Carol Dweck's book "*Mindset: The New Psychology of Success.*" Dweck explains that individuals with a growth mindset perceive their abilities as malleable qualities rather than fixed traits, embracing the belief that continuous effort and learning can nurture and expand their capabilities. Those with a growth mindset exhibit a positive attitude towards learning, willingly take on challenges, and demonstrate resilience in the face of obstacles or setbacks. Sure does sound like the profile of a great startup investor.

To facilitate investors in acquiring knowledge and understanding the concepts of abundance and fixed mindsets, I have structured and organized them into eight (8) clear, specific thematic blocks that align directly with the mindset characteristics of startup investors that I have personally embraced and have seen my most trusted and respected investor colleagues demonstrate. Enriched with data, informed by leadership research, and drawing upon parallels from industries employing analogous frameworks, these thematic blocks serve as a purposeful guide for investors, empowering them to foster and sustain a growth-oriented mindset that drives optimal performance and sustained impact. (Figure 6 – Embracing a Growth Mindset for Startup Investors):

1. **Intelligence, Skills & Abilities.** Emphasizing a commitment to ongoing improvement, investors can actively pursue opportunities for self-development, skill-building, knowledge acquisition, and personal growth by forging engaged connections with all stakeholders within the startup community. Intelligence, skills, and abilities are dynamic and can be continually developed and enhanced. This posture contrasts the fixed mindset of these qualities being static, set, innate, and pre-determined to be finite and limiting. Investors need to employ a long-term perspective and stay motivated by the process of growth rather than solely focusing on immediate outcomes or the destination of an exit. The journey is rich in expanding comprehension and awareness of investing to be better equipped to make decisions with a startup's limited actual traction and revenue.

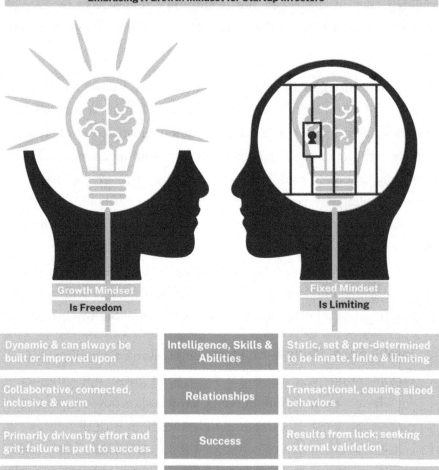

Embracing A Growth Mindset for Startup Investors

Growth Mindset Is Freedom		Fixed Mindset Is Limiting
Dynamic & can always be built or improved upon	Intelligence, Skills & Abilities	Static, set & pre-determined to be innate, finite & limiting
Collaborative, connected, inclusive & warm	Relationships	Transactional, causing siloed behaviors
Primarily driven by effort and grit; failure is path to success	Success	Results from luck; seeking external validation
Learn & grow from to discover areas of improvement	Feedback	A personal attack or criticism on self-worth, thus ignored
Through effort, ability is learned, a path to mastery	Effort	Pointless, futile, lack of ability is predetermined
There is always a way for everyone to win	Negotiation	Zero-sum thoughts: "I win, you lose or you win and I lose"
An opportunity to grow and evolve to be better	Failure	A true threat to hide, conceal & dismiss deficiencies
Purposeful, shared, sum of all strengths & self-monitored	Authority & Power	Stratified, hierarchical & closely controlled

Figure 6

© She Invests! 2023

2. **Relationships.** Investors with a growth mindset prioritize building solid relationships with entrepreneurs, fellow investors, and key stakeholders in the startup ecosystem. They understand that fostering trust, open communication, and mutual respect are vital for effective collaboration and evergreen partnerships. Investors can create a supportive and collaborative network that enhances their knowledge, resources, and opportunities by actively investing in relationship building. Investors who strive to create a warm and supporting network typically provide constructive feedback and guidance to help founders realize their potential. Investors prioritize empathy and understanding, acknowledging that startups are ventures fueled by passion and dedication. By doing so, they foster stronger relationships, inspire loyalty, and cultivate a culture of camaraderie. This approach stands in stark contrast to a fixed mindset that views relationships as transactional, stale, and stagnant, leading to siloed behaviors.

3. **Success.** Success is a result of effort, hard work, and grit. Investors embracing a growth mindset hold the belief that their skills and abilities can be cultivated and enhanced through persistent effort, deliberate practice, and an ongoing commitment to learning. They understand that putting in the effort, seeking improvement, throwing ego out the door, and persisting through the peaks and valleys of the startup journey will allow portfolios to grow. In addition, other people's achievements are viewed as inspirational and motivation rather than feeling threatened or envious. Investors can appreciate and learn from the achievements of the entire startup community ecosystem. Investors should acknowledge the uniqueness of each individual's journey and embrace challenges with a willingness to venture beyond their comfort zones. Investors

understand that tackling new and demanding tasks presents an opportunity to develop new skills, expand their capabilities, foster personal and professional improvement, and thrive in the process.

4. **Feedback.** Embrace a learning mindset and actively seek feedback with a posture of openness and a willingness to grow. By doing so, investors can uncover areas for improvement, gain valuable insights, and enhance their decision-making abilities, ultimately leading to a more informed and vibrant portfolio. Investors who value the input and perspectives of others continually seek guidance and mentoring to enhance their own skills and abilities. Investors should avoid egocentrically dismissing feedback or succumbing to negative self-talk, refraining from perceiving feedback as a personal attack. Instead, they can approach feedback with an open mind, recognizing its immense potential to enhance their overall startup investment journey.

5. **Effort.** Attaining mastery demands dedicated effort and unwavering perseverance. Investors must demonstrate a willingness to invest in the necessary work, navigate obstacles with persistence, and remain steadfast in their pursuit, even in the face of setbacks. Investors can view effort as a means to improve and reach higher levels of awareness and knowledge of the investment world's intricacies. This ability and willingness to learn can be a significant risk mitigation strategy for the ongoing sustainability of a portfolio. The contrary belief suggests that learning is futile and pointless due to a predetermined lack of ability.

6. **Negotiation.** Investors should accept the view that ample opportunities exist for all parties involved to attain mutually beneficial outcomes (a win-win-win scenario), secure favorable deals, facilitate smoother co-investments, and establish a network aligned

with shared values. This perspective can manifest in a founder-friendly approach to term negotiations. However, it is wider than that, as there are also ways to negotiate terms and address investor-friendly needs. For example, priorities of information rights are salient to investors, while priorities of a realistic valuation are critical for founders; yet both sides share the goal of profitability. For investors and entrepreneurs, aiming for understanding and a path forward (because it's a long one) increases a positive outcome. The zero-sum thought of "I win, you lose" or "you win, I lose" is not fruitful in this startup investment industry.

7. **Failure.** Obstacles are a natural part of trying something new or testing a hypothesis, leading to proficiency at some point. Embracing failure as a chance to learn, grow, and evolve, rather than becoming discouraged by it, investors can view failure as a stepping stone toward more substantial alignment with their investment thesis. Investors comprehend that mistakes and setbacks are inherent in the dynamic startup landscape and recognize them as invaluable feedback for personal and professional growth. They analyze failures, extract lessons from them, and use that knowledge to adjust their approach and try again; thus, iteratively designing a purposeful and prosperous investment journey. This viewpoint is essentially unlike the fixed mindset, which perceives failure as a genuine threat to conceal and dismiss any shortcomings.

8. **Authority & Power.** The influential terms "authority" and "power," which bestow investors an advantageous position within the startup ecosystem, can be harnessed for positive impact when they are purposeful, shared, subject to self-monitoring, and viewed as the collective culmination of strengths. Investors should constantly remind themselves that their involvement in a business endeavor

profoundly influences people's dreams and lives. Demonstrating respect, even when encountering a flawed idea or a less-than-stellar pitch, entails refraining from the immediate dismissal of the founder. Instead, offering constructive, actionable, and purposeful feedback is crucial for fostering growth and guiding the founder toward improvement. As an investor, one occupies, by design, a position of power within the startup community. Hence, conducting business with integrity, grace, and humility holds greater influence, recognizing that true impact lies in giving more than receiving, the collective strength and collaborative approach, rather than individual prowess alone. In contrast, adopting a fixed mindset characterized by stratified, hierarchical, and tightly controlled authority and power dilutes investor influence.

A growth mindset for investors aims for strength, vulnerability, and openness, while a fixed mindset shoots for limiting beliefs, guarded postures, and closed demeanors. It is perceived that these two opposing mindsets are similar to the abundance and scarcity philosophies; the abundance mindset aligns with the growth mindset, while the scarcity mindset corresponds to the fixed mindset. This is very true. Consequently, as investors evolve and broaden their perspectives, embracing abundance in mentoring efforts, investment decisions, and network building will undeniably cultivate a growth mindset in their approach to investing. Within a scarcity mindset, investors tend to focus on an investment's constraints, fixate on a founding team's shortcomings, and analyze the limitations of the business model. Funders often hesitate to take calculated risks and could miss out on a startup investing opportunity by adopting a narrow perspective regarding their own investor journey. Be abundant in investing in startups with a strong growth mindset, avoiding the scarcity mindset with fixed or restricted beliefs.

Practically speaking, a worthwhile approach to transition from a scarcity to an abundance mindset daily is actively engaging with, listening to, and reciting money mantras. Throughout my own investment journey, I have consistently tried to embrace an abundance mindset, but honestly, it is tough when the journey gets challenging. These mantras serve as anchors, guiding me towards my north star of maintaining an abundance mindset, albeit in an uncertain startup investor world. By repeating them consistently, I realign my focus and quickly shift away from the scarcity mindset mantras that sometimes consume my mind. Instead, I embrace abundance mindset mantras, transforming negative thoughts into positive affirmations that empower and uplift me. (See Figure 7 – The Startup Investor Mindset Mantras)

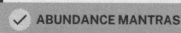

The Startup Investor Mindset Mantras

✓ ABUNDANCE MANTRAS	✗ SCARCITY MANTRAS
• I embrace the exhilarating challenge of self-improvement	• I don't like to be challenged because it scares me
• Failure is an opportunity to grow	• Failure is the limit of my abilities
• If you succeed, I am inspired	• If you succeed, I feel threatened
• Feedback helps me move forward & grow	• Feedback is a critique about me personally
• My effort and attitude are malleable & impact everything	• My abilities & assets determine everything, I have no influence
• Asking questions will help me learn & gain clarity	• Asking questions makes me look unintelligent & stupid
• I lead with inclusivity, openness, transparency, and empathy	• I lead with power, position, and top-down authority
• I possess the ability to learn anything I put my mind to	• I am either good at it or not, I have no power to change

© She Invests! 2023

Figure 7

The world of startup investing can be frustrating, confusing, and emotional. Investors might not see an exit for seven years, they might have passed on an investment that became Spanx, Canva, 23 and Me, Airwallex, Glossier, Nextdoor, or Canva (all women-led unicorns), or they might experience five startups fail in a row that were deemed great investments. The resilience, grit, patience, and determination will get an investor through the journey with mental fortitude, a growth mindset, and a network of like-minded startup advocates.

iv. Embodying Long-Term Thinking and Patience

Essential qualities of early-stage investors include adopting a long-term perspective for return on investment over the span of multiple years and actively supporting the startup team in achieving their milestones. Patience is fundamental in cultivating this mindset and aligning investors' financial horizons with the entrepreneur's vision and proposed timelines. Given that startups typically require time to mature and flourish into thriving businesses, it is crucial for investors, who play an integral role in the company's journey, to prioritize nurturing growth.

Tolerant investors recognize that it takes time for startups to iterate and refine their products, establish market presence, hone business models, acquire customers, generate meaningful revenues, and clarify strategies to find the optimal fit in the market. This essential time horizon builds a valuable and sustainable business that delights customers and produces sustainable long-term value over time, ensuring, under the uncertain circumstances of a startup, the most successful outcomes over the startup's journey toward an exit. In honor of innovation and lean strategy, investors with a long-term horizon approach allow for ongoing iteration and learning; thus understanding that failures and pivots are part of the compounding effect of the startup's steady progress.

Lastly, as an external consideration, having a long-term approach allows investors to better weather market fluctuations. They understand that short-term market volatility does not necessarily reflect the long-term potential of a startup. The journey of startups is marked by roller-coaster-like fluxes in revenue, with soaring highs and challenging lows. Partnerships that once held promise can falter unexpectedly, and reliance on certain manufacturers may prove unreliable. Furthermore, customer buying habits can shift abruptly, ongoing fundraising avenues can suddenly dry up, or the market can take unexpected turns. The unpredictable nature of the startup landscape demands resilience and adaptability from entrepreneurs as they navigate through a dynamic and ever-changing business environment. Startup investors prioritizing long-term value creation over short-term gains are willing to forgo immediate liquidity or quick exits if it aligns with the long-term sustainability of an impactful startup, undeniably counter-culture, at times, to the buzz of the startup environment.

V. Embracing Uncertainty and Ambiguity

Startup investors embrace uncertainty and ambiguity, acknowledging the risks involved in early-stage investments. They adapt to changing circumstances, revise strategies, and seize new opportunities. Embracing failure as part of the learning process, investors understand that not all investments will succeed and view failures as learning opportunities. Investors assess the upside against risks, knowing startup investments take time to deliver returns. By actively engaging with the innovation ecosystem, these investors enhance the certainty of their continued success through collaboration, forming valuable connections, and effectively mobilizing additional capital. Investors are then empowered with impactful insights, trends, and opportunities that contribute to well-informed decision-making and the advancement of their investment goals.

Furthermore, these forward-thinking investors exhibit a remarkable ability to manage uncertainty adeptly. They recognize that embracing volatility does not imply a lack of caution or reckless behavior. This balance ensures that they allocate capital wisely and maintain a diversified portfolio.

Chapter 3

Developing an Investment Thesis

Having a clear vision of the startups that captivate an investor's interest provides clarity for entrepreneurs, a sense of focus for co-investors, and strengthens the conviction of ecosystem advocates who are instrumental partners in the investor's journey. To truly embrace the purposeful investor mindset, remember:

- ⊙ To be patient rather than impulsive
- ⊙ To be realistic rather than overconfident
- ⊙ To be prudent rather than reckless
- ⊙ To be methodical rather than impulsive
- ⊙ To be relational rather than transactional
- ⊙ To be aware of the long time horizon rather than seeking a quick win
- ⊙ To be paying it forward rather than taking it all in
- ⊙ To be growth-minded rather than limited

i. Conviction and Decision-Making

Constructing a robust and tailored investment thesis that aligns with personal goals and beliefs in parallel to the long-term mission of a startup, along with building conviction and sharpening decision-making skills as an investor, encourages and promotes the startup economy to thrive. For startup investors, conviction signifies an unwavering belief in the immense potential of a specific investment opportunity. Investors with conviction possess remarkable clarity of vision regarding the startup's capacity to prosper, the value it can generate, and the significant impact it can make in the market. This conviction stems from a thorough understanding of the startup's business model, competitive landscape, industry trends, and the alignment of the investment opportunity with the investor's investment thesis and goals.

Investors' conviction and strong decision-making can significantly influence the entrepreneurial teams they back. Startups often look to their investors for guidance, mentorship, and strategic input. Investors with conviction can inspire confidence and motivate entrepreneurs, fostering a strong partnership built on shared vision and goals. This alignment strengthens the relationship between investors and entrepreneurs, leading to better collaboration, decision-making, and execution.

Startup investing involves making decisions based on limited information and forecasted outcomes. Investors with solid convictions can analyze available data, perform due diligence, assess risks, act decisively, allocate resources effectively, and promptly make well-informed decisions. Lastly, investors with conviction can effectively communicate their investment thesis and rally resources around their chosen startups. They can inspire other investors, potential partners, and key stakeholders by articulating a compelling vision and demonstrating a deep understanding of the market opportunity. Conviction and confidence in decision-making attract like-minded individuals and resources, creating a substantial support network for the startup; all providing additional capital, expertise, strategic guidance, and valuable connections.

ii. Constructing a Startup Investment Thesis

What is an investment thesis? A roadmap for investing. GRAVITY. It guides the investor towards investments that fit their financial objectives. An investment thesis is a crucial guide for investors to maintain discipline and focus on startups that align with their investment objectives. Without an investment thesis, investors may struggle to stay on track, risk wasting time sourcing and evaluating misaligned startup companies, and end up engaging in unproductive discussions with unsuitable individuals. An investment thesis serves as a guiding compass not only for investors but also helps entrepreneurs navigate their way to investors for guidance, advice, and funding. It also provides stakeholders in the startup ecosystem with insights into the investors' guiding principles, enabling others to join them along the transformative journey.

As one of the most valuable and insightful tools in the innovation economy, the investment thesis guides, connects, and clarifies. It informs investors' deal-sourcing strategies, shapes critical decision-making processes, and ultimately aids in constructing a diversified, impactful, and expanding portfolio. From angel investors having their own personal statements to angel groups developing a collective affirmation to VC funds. This simple yet impactful statement should be used as a trust-building tool. For investors, a robust thesis keeps objectives clear instead of becoming enamored with a charismatic founder and investing in a deal that they cannot bring any value to and, thus, should not be investing in.

A good investment thesis intersects experience, aspirations, assets, passion, values, and opportunity, fitting the financial objectives and goals of the investor. Nevertheless, it's essential to be mindful of the unconscious biases ingrained in our society from an early age regarding what patterns of "success" to favor. Remembering the importance of diversification can help navigate these biases and make more balanced and informed investment decisions. Pattern recognition is a natural cognitive process we all engage in daily. In the rapid evaluation of startups, investors rely on pattern recognition to identify potential "winners." Similarly, patterns are engrained around the ideal founder-funder pairs like Donald Valentine, founder of Sequoia Capital, who invested in Atari in 1975 after meeting Steve Jobs, who was, at that time, a line engineer for Atari. Suppose investors come across an entrepreneur who resembles a younger version of themselves or someone like a successful founder such as Mark Zuckerberg of Meta. In that case, they are more inclined to invest. Over 75% of angel investors and 95% of VCs are male. However, when faced with an entrepreneur who is a woman or a person of color, they may not see the same familiar patterns and tend to be more hesitant to invest.

Unconscious biases come to the forefront, hindering access to capital, limiting opportunities, and resulting in decreased diversity of thought and ideas. Pattern recognition is bias turned practice. When driven by bias, pattern recognition becomes a barrier to inclusivity and equity in the startup ecosystem.

The consequence of these biases is the perpetuation of the status quo, with a limited range of founders and startups being given the opportunity to thrive. Such homogeneity stifles innovation and limits the potential for breakthrough ideas to emerge. Investors with a purposeful mindset of impact recognize the significance of breaking this cycle and seek to challenge the dominant patterns. They are committed to funding a new narrative that celebrates the impactful and resilient stories of diverse markets, innovative new products, and emerging founders.

By embracing diversity and investing in founders from underrepresented communities, these purposeful investors redefine the notion of "success" in the startup world. They champion startups led by women, people of color, and individuals from diverse backgrounds, acknowledging that greatness and potential are not confined to specific patterns; talent is everywhere, opportunity is not. Instead, they celebrate the richness and strength that diversity brings to the entrepreneurial landscape. These forward-thinking investors empower exceptional founders, regardless of background or identity, to redefine possibilities and shatter existing norms.

Investors can also effectively diversify various other factors when funding, such as geography, business models, technology, or customer segments, by focusing on a specific industry or sector they are familiar with. This approach facilitates the development of a well-balanced investment portfolio tailored to align with an investor's personal net worth. Developing a personal investment thesis will guide investors toward what they want to invest their time, treasure, and talent into. This alignment is magnified as it not only shows other investors to discover, collaborate, and syndicate deals but also leads to identifying more values-aligned opportunities.

To aid in crafting a compelling investment thesis, most investors employ a standard formula that defines their thesis quickly and efficiently. The typical formula for an investment thesis is as follows: (Figure 8 – The Startup Investment Thesis)

"I invest in [typical founder profile]
with a typical investment of [typical check size]
at the [typical stage of company] stage
in [geography]
to fund startups in [sector/market]
with [Secret Sauce]."

Investors can add further insight as necessary, like:

- ⊙ **"I provide** [assets you can bring to the company] **to all portfolio companies because I am** [your background/interest] **to** [Secret Sauce].
- ⊙ **I like to** [how do you interact with companies/founders], **I** [prefer/not prefer] **a board seed, and request** [typical asks of founders, like information rights, etc.]
- ⊙ **I look for liquidity in less than** [typical horizon of investment periods].

To enhance knowledge sharing regarding the distinctions among investment theses of individual angels, angel groups, and venture funds, exemplifying the interdependencies and interconnectedness of the startup community, here are three illustrations.

1. As an angel investor who has backed more than 140 companies, my personal investment thesis states:

"I invest in women-led or BIPOC-led startups in the seed round, typically $25,000 each deal. I am industry agnostic but prefer tech-enabled solutions. I focus on looking for difficult problems that I believe can be solved with the right team; I am founder-first. I can either lead a round if it is in my wheelhouse of expertise or follow on. I like to take an active role in advising the founder(s), prefer a board seat, but not necessary, and request information rights. I look for a liquidity event in 3-5 years and 5-7 years for life science." (BIPOC: Black, Indigenous, People of Color)

2. As the founder and leader of Stella Angels, an angel group comprising over 45 investors, our investment thesis revolves around:

"Stella Angels is a predominantly women angel network whose passion is to invest in women entrepreneurs. Stella Angels invests in diverse women-led startups in the pre-seed and seed round, typically either as a collective SPV (Special Purpose Vehicle) with a combined minimum check size of $50K or individually ($5K to $100K). The group is industry agnostic, requests information rights, and conducts due diligence as a group or organized by leadership from Stella Foundation."

3. The investment thesis of Stella Impact Capital, the fund for which I am a General Partner, reads like this:

"Stella Impact Capital is a $50MM seed stage venture fund in the United States to back diverse women-led, deep tech, impact-driven companies led by a team managing 150+ investments, 6 exits, and 1 IPO."

Now that there is a framework to create and examples to inspire, here are five steps to create your investment thesis:

1. **Analyze your successes and failures critically.** What are you good at? Where have you been effective, and where have you encountered challenges? In which areas have you demonstrated significant effectiveness, and in which areas have you faced challenges or limitations? Write these down, take note – both successes and failures – acknowledging them as valuable experiences. Doing so allows you to leverage your triumphs to further progress and avoid repeating past challenges. Learn through careful evaluation.

2. **Be acutely aware of your strengths.** What are the areas in which you excel and possess notable strengths? Do you understand markets, personalities, or technology? What is it that you do best in the life cycle of a business, from idea to exit? Take a specific and comprehensive approach by creating a list, regardless of length, highlighting the unique contributions and skills you bring to a business. To delve deeper into identifying your strengths, consider taking the Gallup© StrengthsFinder test (https://www.gallup.com/cliftonstrengths), which can provide valuable insights into your unique personal strengths in the four talent themes: Executing, Strategic Thinking, Influencing, and Relationship Building.

3. **Get super specific with your thesis.** Ensure utmost specificity in crafting your investment thesis, precisely defining the criteria, focus areas, and objectives to guide your investment decisions. Having absolute clarity enables investors to provide adequate support to the entrepreneurs they fund, thereby exerting a more efficient influence on and shaping the market of interest. Specificity allows investors to stand out in the crowd. Investors want their peers (i.e., co-investors, syndication partners, and angels in network) to be able to say, "She only does XYZ kind of deal." Investors strive to establish a distinct and precise reputation for their specific expertise and focus areas in the investment world. This approach is similar to creating SMART goals that are Specific, Measurable, Attainable, Realistic, and Time-bound.

4. **Test and iterate your thesis.** The validation of an investor's thesis involves benchmarking it against the dynamics of a thriving innovation ecosystem, the prevailing broad economic conditions, and the existing financial landscape in the private markets, thus

ensuring its relevance and effectiveness. Iterate and validate an investment thesis by also actively testing it with startups that align with its core criteria. Pressure test it in the "real world." Purposefully engaging in discussions with startup advocates and seeking feedback from institutional or corporate VCs (the next set of investors in the funding pipeline) can provide valuable insights and assistance in validating and refining an investment thesis, enhancing its robustness and applicability in the market. For aspiring investors, honing in on the specific startup of interest, akin to defining a buyer persona, brings clarity to the investment journey. Conversely, existing investors can benefit from identifying the exemplary startup within their portfolio that epitomizes their investment thesis, serving as a guiding reference point, further strengthening the investor's focus and strategic approach.

5. **Collaborate on streamlined deal flow.** Share deals/investment opportunities and build trust among peers. Foster collaborative relationships with fellow investors to establish a robust network that facilitates streamlined deal flow. Embrace a continuous learning mindset, remaining open to new insights and perspectives that can enhance investment decision-making and contribute to long-term success. Be willing to learn and include all stakeholders for maximum return on sourcing efforts.

As a versatile tool, the investment thesis can evolve and undergo refinement as investors expand their portfolios and engage in meaningful conversations with diverse founders, funders, and ecosystem builders. This ongoing process allows investors to gain valuable insights and adjust their investment thesis to align with emerging market trends, evolving community opportunities, and changing economic dynamics.

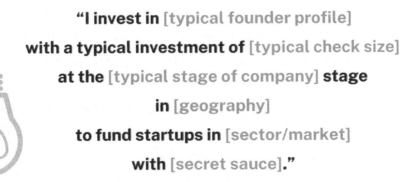

© She Invests! 2023

Figure 8

iii. The Investment Thesis Supports Transparency

A clear investment thesis signals professionalism, intentionality, openness, and reciprocity to an investor's growing innovation community, from other investors to entrepreneurs to service providers to mentors. Transparency and trust are intricately connected in the investment world. By increasing transparency, an investor can also:

1. **Increase adequate deal flow.** The quality and quantity of deal flow that an investor directly influences the strength of a growing portfolio. Great deal flow often arrives from angel investors, angel groups, venture capitalists, accelerator directors, and other early-stage investors. Relationships must be synergistic and open for the proper deal flow to effortlessly infuse the investor's radar.

2. **Assist syndication efforts.** When an investor engages in syndication, collaborating and sharing exceptional deals with other investors or within their angel group, it facilitates an exchange of value. A quick definition of syndication. Angel syndicates are membership groups that collaborate and commune through promoting and presenting investment opportunities to their members, albeit individual investors, angel groups, or funds. Syndicates typically efficiently handle deal flow, due diligence, and transactions (like treaties or agreements for sharing reports or information amongst its members) for their investor network. Members then have the freedom to decide whether to invest their personal funds in the companies. Certain angel syndicates also operate independent funds, providing opportunities for joint investments alongside their member investors. Through collaborative connectivity, investors reinforce a sense of assurance in syndication, exemplified by practical and actionable steps taken in the deal-making process to achieve the most productive outcomes.

3. **Saves time.** A well-prepared investment thesis saves valuable time by providing clear guidance on the types of investments a funder seeks, enabling the larger ecosystem to easily understand how to bring value to an investor and vice versa. This streamlined approach fosters efficient communication and collaboration, facilitating

meaningful interactions that align with specific investment objectives and enhance the startup network's overall value exchange.

4. **Better communication with co-investors.** A focused investment thesis facilitates richer communications and fosters cross-collaboration with co-investors throughout the entire investment journey, from sourcing syndication deals to eventual exit or sale. This alignment of investment goals and shared understanding cultivates stronger relationships, enhances knowledge sharing, and enables seamless coordination among co-investors. This approach ultimately maximizes the potential for collective growth and aggregate value creation.

It is crucial to keep in mind that early-stage investments inherently carry a degree of risk, and even ventures with the most brilliant ideas, polished and perfected products, ideal product-market fit, and exceptional teams can still face failure. Establishing a systematic approach to assist investors in evaluating outstanding and passionate entrepreneurs and their transformative products is critical. An investment thesis will decrease risk as an investor and increase the probability of investment outcomes aligned to their own beliefs and experience.

Do not rush it. Investors should invest in the innovation and impact they want to see in the world. Developing and refining a personal investment thesis as an early-stage investor should take thought, research, and time. Factors to consider:

⊙ Without an investment thesis, investors will likely find it challenging to stay disciplined and concentrate on the startups that match their investment objectives. **Get clear.**

> Without an investment thesis, investors don't have an intentional compass to guide their deal flow sourcing and make the best investment decisions. **Get focused.**

> Without an investment thesis, investors will likely waste a lot of time talking about the wrong things to the wrong people. **Get aligned.**

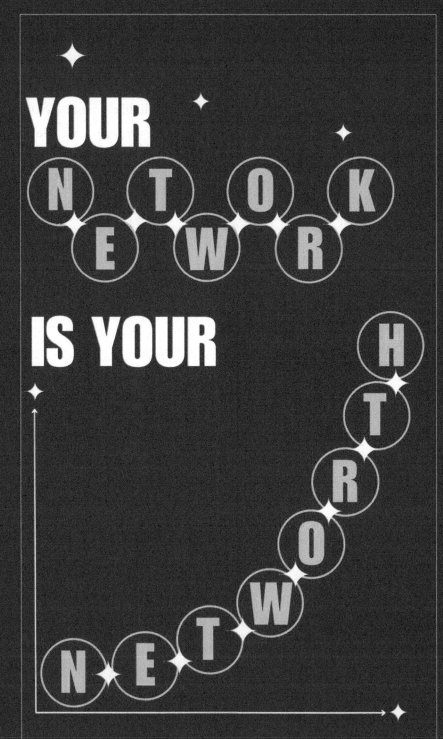

Chapter 4

Growing Influence and Impact

An investor's network is their net worth. This is deeply ingrained in the minds of individuals in leadership positions. A startup investor naturally grows their influence and impact as they write checks and build their portfolio, pouring into their pockets and purpose. Mindful investors transcend the realm of financial investment and wield indirect and direct influence to actively shape and empower the entrepreneurs and ecosystems with which they engage. They proactively contribute their expertise, networks, and resources to support the growth and development of startups, thereby fostering a positive and impactful environment that catalyzes innovation and drives collective success.

The concept of defining impact has long intrigued and bewildered economists, leading them to explore various dimensions and perspectives in their exceptional dissertations and research. Attempting to grasp the true essence of impact has not only been intellectually stimulating, but has also provided valuable insights into understanding the far-reaching implications of economic decisions and policies. Economists' exploration of impact has shed light on the complex interplay of factors that shape societies, industries, and global economies, making their contributions invaluable in the pursuit of sustainable development and equitable progress.

In our modern age of social media and captivating short-form videos that consume hours of scrolling, the term "influence" has become synonymous with "social influencers." However, for the purposes of this startup investor guide, influence takes on a more amorphous nature, encompassing the dynamic interplay between power, humility, authority, and a commitment to serving the greater good. It extends beyond mere popularity to embody the ability to effect positive change and make a meaningful impact on ventures, industries, and society as a whole.

Through their intentional involvement, purposeful investors become catalysts for positive change, leaving a lasting imprint on the entrepreneurial journey and the overall innovation landscape. The impact of resourced capital coupled with network influence beyond funding captivates the entire community to give, get, and go. It forms a virtuous economic development and growth cycle as impactful investors reinvest their resources and expertise back into the community. Simultaneously, exited entrepreneurs contribute their knowledge and wealth, creating a symbiotic relationship that fuels further innovation, job creation, and prosperity.

i. Learning and Continuous Improvement

Embracing a culture of continuous learning cultivates an investor who is knowledgeable, versatile, and adept at confidently navigating uncertainty, enabling them to make informed investment decisions and allocate their capital wisely towards innovative startups. Continuously immersing oneself in market research, staying updated on emerging trends, and exploring new frontiers of opportunity through dedicated reading and active listening becomes a rewarding use of an investor's free time. This perpetual learning mindset ensures they stay relevant, refreshed, and well-positioned to leverage their competitive edge in the ever-evolving market landscape. Gaining insights from seasoned investors is paramount in cultivating a diverse range of profiles and stories that enrich decision-making processes.

Insights and wisdom shared by successful investors are always nuggets of new knowledge worth absorbing in books, audible guides, LinkedIn newsletters, Youtube channels, and podcasts. Podcasts are excellent for investors to dive into: *The Angel Next Door* podcast by Marcia Dawood has exceptional stories, *This Week in Startups* by Jason Calacanis inspires through unicorn companies and the investors who fund them, *She Invests!* podcast by Dr. Silvia Mah (me) and my fabulous women investor guests, and *The Twenty Minute VC* by Harry Stebbings gives insight into later-stage investors and their mindsets). This exposure to the experiences of others enables aspiring and veteran investors to gain valuable insights, navigate potential pitfalls, and make informed decisions.

Investors acquire knowledge and insights through various channels and methods, so it is crucial to identify and prioritize the most enjoyable and effective forms of learning that resonate. Whether it's reading books, attending conferences, participating in webinars, engaging in mentorship programs, coffee meetings, various in person and virtual panels, Angel Capital Association webinars, investor summits like Womens Venture Summit by Stella Foundation, or networking with industry professionals, investors can embracing their preferred learning avenues to enhance the learning experience and facilitates deeper understanding.

THERE ARE MANY PATHS TO TAKE

Investors can proactively approach finding the best innovations by becoming knowledgeable about leading through uncertainty, understanding new business models, recruiting and developing great teams, creating diversification and redundancy in portfolio management, or analyzing industry trends. Investors should actively seek information that supports both entrepreneurs who may encounter challenges and investors who require guidance when evaluating a startup. This balanced approach promotes a comprehensive understanding of the investment landscape. Thus, investments are made in the most fruitful context of a trending market and eager customers.

ii. Providing Value-Added Support, Championing, and Mentorship

Establishing genuine and meaningful connections with founders and their teams, both pre- and post-investment, fosters the creation of a profound and robust value chain that generates mutual benefits for all parties involved. As an investor, it is imperative to embrace a posture of wholehearted engagement and transparency, bringing a full-self approach to support and empower the entrepreneurs within your portfolio, enhancing the potential of meaningful collaborations and long-term growth. Bringing to the table internal assets like empathy, leadership, discernment, listening skills, personal experiences, and a true heart for championing the entrepreneur is equally vital as bringing outward-facing resources like networks, introductions, and connections. This relationship-building starts even before the investment is penned. Shepherding a strong relationship with the founders allows for valuable insights to be obtained into their vision, strategic direction, and core values, enabling a deeper understanding of their business, operations, and future growth strategies. This exploration can also help investors assess the startup team's ability to execute the business plan. How to do this?

Investors can showcase their dedication to truly champion entrepreneurs by engaging in tactical value-add activities like company site visits, collaboratively providing assistance reviewing documents through the due diligence process, attending meetings to gain insights on internal culture, external customer relations, and partnerships, and conducting multifaceted connectivity opportunities to build trust.

Investors can proactively schedule site visits to gain organic connectivity with the entrepreneurial team and better understand operations. By physically visiting the company's premises, investors gain unprecedented intel by engaging with the team in their element, interacting with the innovation, albeit manufacturing a consumer product or a customer site where the technology is in use, and experiencing the company's culture firsthand. Investors can develop a deeper understanding of the startup's operations, build stronger relationships with the founders and their growing team, and gain valuable on-the-ground insights and experiences.

Active involvement by investors in reviewing business documents with the entrepreneurial team during due diligence showcases commitment to synergy and cooperation. This collaborative approach not only strengthens the investor-founder relationship during the investment process but also sets the foundation for effective investor relations and ongoing communication after the investment. By actively participating in this collaborative review method, investors can ask relevant questions, dive into specific verticals of interest with curiosity, confirm assumptions with grace, assess strengths and risks with empathy, and provide valuable insights with open-mindedness. Nurturing this environment that fosters transparency and trust promotes stronger connections among stakeholders. Investors demonstrate their dedication to understanding the startup's operations, contributing their expertise, and fostering a sense of true reciprocity of value with the founders, ultimately leading to a more productive and mutually beneficial long-term relationship.

Attending startup meetings allows investors to immerse themselves in the startup's internal culture and witness firsthand how the team communicates and operates for overall effectiveness. Additionally, attending meetings with customers or clients (if appropriate) provides investors with a deeper understanding of the startup's market positioning, customer interactions, and the value the product or service delivers. This direct experience strengthens the investor's relationship with the startup and enables them to make more informed assessments of its growth potential and alignment with their investment thesis.

Investors can leverage various connectivity tactics to engage with founders and build strong relationships that I call micro-moments of connection. These tactics include engaging in casual conversations over coffee to connect at a deeper level or invite other investors to join the journey, engaging in walking get-to-know-you talks to foster a relaxed and open environment, participating in group experiences such as celebrating significant milestones achieved by the startup or attending panel events where the founder is speaking. By utilizing these diverse approaches, investors create multiple touchpoints for meaningful interactions, enabling them to gain deeper insights into the founder's vision, values, and aspirations. This multifaceted connectivity enhances the investor-founder relationship, fosters trust and rapport, and facilitates a more comprehensive understanding of the startup's potential for long-term impact and viability.

Championing entrepreneurs to other investors goes beyond financial support and creates a powerful sense of connection between the entrepreneur's fundraising goals and the investor's expanding startup portfolio. Still, it also plays a vital role in fostering a thriving ecosystem of support and collaboration. By actively advocating for the entrepreneurs they have invested in, investors become ambassadors of their vision, potential, and achievements. By sharing positive experiences, insights, and recommendations with fellow investors, the champion investor not only amplifies the visibility of the entrepreneur and their venture but also helps to build credibility and trust within the investor community. Equally, by communicating progress updates on investor relations, private market insights, and relevant industry trends, these same investors can inspire confidence and generate interest amongst the most investable entrepreneurs and their colleagues, ultimately leading to stronger strategic partnerships and additional values-aligned investment opportunities.

This act of championing creates a virtuous cycle where prosperous entrepreneurs, thriving investor portfolios, and noteworthy investor-entrepreneur journeys attract more interest and potential capital activation, cultivating a supportive network that celebrates achievements and encourages further innovation. Additionally, it strengthens the investor's reputation as a trusted advisor and resource within the startup community, positioning them as a valued connector and influencer in the investment industry. As more investors witness the positive outcomes of these collaborative partnerships, they become inspired to participate in the startup ecosystem, contributing to its overall expansion and generating even more opportunities for entrepreneurs to thrive. Ultimately, this collective effort fuels a continuous cycle of positive outcomes, driving economic growth and creating a dynamic environment for innovation and entrepreneurship.

Lastly, it is worth noting that the concept of mentorship has become commonplace in the startup community. While many investors express their willingness to provide guidance and support, it is crucial to recognize the significance of financial backing for entrepreneurs in their journey to scale. Rather than seeking repetitive mentorship, entrepreneurs require funding that enables them to propel their ventures to the next level. This conundrum highlights the importance of balancing mentorship and financial investment, ensuring entrepreneurs receive the necessary resources to accelerate their growth.

I encourage investors to mentor entrepreneurs who can use their expertise in concrete and validating ways; dig in to dive deep. This type of mentoring brings an entrepreneur closer to an inflection point that might provide revenue-generating opportunities, making the startup more investable and reducing the need for further excessive funding. That is a true value-add for that entrepreneur and can prove to be a vital element in an investor's sourcing equation and ongoing due diligence.

I strongly advocate and encourage investors to engage in impactful mentoring relationships with entrepreneurs who can genuinely benefit from their specific expertise and guidance in practical and validating ways. If I sound like a broken record, then, write the check!

WRITE

THE

CHECK

Investors can also encourage capital efficiency to keep the power of progress in the hands of founders. By delving deep into the challenges and opportunities of the startup, this focused and targeted mentoring approach can propel entrepreneurs towards significant milestones (a "check the box" goal) and pivotal inflection points (a multifaceted point that substantially changes the valuation, perception, or velocity of a startup). This approach motivates founders to achieve revenue-generating success and reduce their reliance on external funding. By actively contributing to the growth and investability of startups through this type of mentoring, investors can add significant value to the entrepreneur's journey and enhance their own sourcing equation and ongoing due diligence process. A win-win for sure!

iii. Network Building and Collaboration

Continually nurturing and deepening trust is crucial for fostering strong relationships between investors, as well as between investors and entrepreneurs, creating an environment where knowledge-sharing thrives and deal flow is enhanced. By establishing a foundation of trust, investors can engage in open and transparent communication, collaborate effectively, and share valuable insights and opportunities. These trusted relationships provide a platform for meaningful engagement, mutual support, and cultivating a vibrant investment ecosystem. Respect and trust are planted with initial conversations and mutual respect, then watered and grown with insights, connections, and collaborations, and then flourished with the radiant light of sustained strengths and rich resources shed by all involved. Purposeful relationships abandon personal ambition, diminish harmful intent and build on collective wisdom, and amplify abundance. Each member of this collective relationship-build devotes their unique intellect, creativity, and talent to the network.

Showing up as investors with integrity for others in an open posture of support and impact creates abundance. I have observed numerous instances of investors collaborating on due diligence teams and exchanging valuable investor updates from portfolio companies (such as in an SPV, Special Purpose Vehicle), offering warm introductions to facilitate co-investments, and advocating for intensional syndication efforts amongst investor groups. These collaborative efforts and assistance among investors showcase the spirit of partnership and the collective drive for true inclusive progress within the startup economy. Don't confuse this idea with outright self-sacrifice; this relationship building is created on confidence in each other, respect for everyone's intellect, and leadership in their respective areas of expertise.

By providing warm introductions, investors contribute to the growth and interconnectedness of the entrepreneurial community, fostering valuable connections not only for entrepreneurs but also for like-minded investors. While deal flow serves as the crown jewel, representing great innovations and talented founders and teams, the cultivation of pipelines is a treasured queen, ensuring a continuous stream of promising opportunities for all stakeholders involved. Connecting investors with co-investors before, during, and after their investment is critical to continued startup viability and portfolio sustainability. When early-stage startups need to raise anywhere between $500K and $1.5M for each of their pre-seed and seed rounds of financing, the power of the investor community needs to be engaged to fill the entire round. In an ideal scenario, existing values-aligned investors already on the cap table extend invitations and encouragement to their like-minded colleagues to contribute value and capital. The more an investor creates a web of influence, creating jungle gyms of support, the stronger the trust becomes while the network grows more rigorous. Community-building is essential for capital to be activated, cultivated by excellent deal flow, shepherded by educational experiences, and amplified by all the voices at the table.

TRUST IS THE MOST VALUABLE CURRENCY IN THE STARTUP ECOSYSTEM

Chapter 5

Building Trust, the Most Valuable Currency of the Innovation Ecosystem

Building trust is the paramount objective of a startup investor, as it not only fosters stronger relationships among stakeholders in the ecosystem, including entrepreneurs and fellow investors, but also acts as the adhesive that enhances deal sourcing, catalyzes innovation, mitigates risks, and amplifies the impact of capital infusion. By cultivating trust with values-aligned entrepreneurs, investors contribute to the ongoing influence and impact of the entire innovation economy.

i. What is Trust?

Trust is something that cannot be seen or touched but brings immense value. It catalyzes action amongst individuals and communities. It's broken when values are challenged. It's fragile yet extremely strong, remarkably resilient, and easily broken when personal values are challenged. It's malleable in every person's definition of trust yet rigid in conviction and strength. Trust is shaped by character, by factors like respect, honesty, accountability and integrity, transparency, and consistency. Trust strengthens personal and business connections. Like an investor thesis, trust should be meticulously examined and defined by startup investors and held to the highest standard in deal negotiations and investing in the high-risk asset class. Establishing trust as a foundational element in investor-entrepreneur relationships fosters progress toward growth inflection points and provides a calming influence amidst uncertainty.

Defining trust can be challenging because its value, influence, and impact is immeasurable. Through years of experience in community building and navigating the investor landscape, I have realized and appreciate the following about trust:

Trust is

Tremendous

Reciprocity

For **U** AND US

with **S**incerity

And **T**ransparency

TREMENDOUS

RECIPROCITY

between

U & US

with

SINCERITY

and

TRANSPARENCY

The first T in Trust: Tremendous.

Establishing and fostering tremendous amounts of trust among individual members of the community is essential to making the currency valuable, as it forms the foundation for meaningful connections and the activation of capital with a shared abundance mindset. Through interviews with over 50 women investors (published on the *She Invests!* podcast) and interactions with hundreds more, it is evident that an abundance mindset drives the collective efforts of early-stage investors to address significant challenges with every connection forged and every carefully deployed capital. Trust serves as our most valuable currency. Furthermore, it demands an immense vision to innovate new products that can disrupt future markets. Investors must forecast and believe wholeheartedly, while entrepreneurs must project and persuade convincingly.

The R in Trust: Reciprocity.

The authentic reciprocation of resources, human capital, and financial capital is the driving force behind the growth and development of a vibrant startup community, fostering a culture of collaboration and partnership. The principle of reciprocity is that of mutual responsiveness, open exchange, and patient exchanges among its stakeholders. Entrepreneurs should reciprocate resources, share connections, reconnect with other founders, and reshare consistently. When investors and ecosystem-builders do the same acts of reciprocity, they create a collaborative environment that nurtures innovation, amplifies influence, and drives meaningful impact. These exchanges in an evergreen feedback loop fuel a supportive community that empowers members to thrive towards mutually positive goals.

The U in Trust: U and Us.

At the core of the trust currency is a simple relationship between U and us, between a single person and the startup collective. This connection transcends individual boundaries and encourages a shared vision for progress. It is a bond built on shared values and mutual support, where each person plays a vital role, contributing their unique and genuine perspectives. Trust weaves a strong thread of interconnectedness among investors, entrepreneurs, and the entire startup community. This trust is nurtured through open communication, transparent dealings, and shared values, creating a powerful synergy that strengthens the fabric of the community. Strengths that are empowered and championed are key. A profound sense of purpose emerges in this mutually dependant ecosystem, where trust and vision converge. Investors and entrepreneurs alike are driven by the shared goal of transforming ideas into reality.

The S in Trust: Sincerity.

Authentic and genuine connections create a profound sense of care among stakeholders. Founders who are approachable and authentic with their customers, investors, and partners cultivate a loyal believers base. When stakeholders feel a strong sense of belonging and care, they naturally become advocates, driven by their unwavering conviction. By sincerely sharing milestones and challenges, entrepreneurs can foster a dedicated community of supporters who rally behind their startups. By openly discussing their journey and co-creating it with interested investors, both the achievements and the hurdles, founders, and funders can create an atmosphere of authenticity and clarity. This sincerity will not only earn entrepreneurs the trust and respect of their community, but it also fosters a sense of camaraderie and collaboration. In this vibrant ecosystem, individuals eagerly offer support, insights, and resources to help startups navigate obstacles and celebrate achievements.

The second T in Trust: Transparency

Maintaining transparency as a guiding principle with investors encourages honest and straightforward interactions but can indeed present challenges. Balancing the need for confidentiality in specific evaluations and negotiations while striving for open communication and disclosure requires careful navigation. Encouraging transparent conversations involves ensuring that statements align with constructive evaluation, genuine thoughts, and appropriate feedback. Along with following through on commitments and promises, credibility is then further strengthened, and trust continues to be built. Transparency may not be the norm in the startup world, but it holds significant potential to foster a purposeful and values-aligned community of investors and entrepreneurs. Embracing true transparency in "comms and ops" (communication and operations), stakeholders can align their actions with their values.

ii. Building Trust Amongst all Startup Ecosystem Stakeholders

Trust and connectivity with ecosystem connectors, entrepreneurs, and other investors who actively engage in activities such as investing, judging pitch competitions, advising founders, mentoring, or offering pitch preparation support are crucial elements in building a thriving startup economy. The currency of trust within this ecosystem is not solely based on financial transactions but instead earned through consistent actions of giving to others, self-minimizing, open communication, delivering on promises, and relationship-building, demonstrating a commitment to the success of the collective. Investors can create a supportive and thriving network by nurturing trust and fostering meaningful connectivity. Leveraging their exceptional juxtaposed position of power and purpose, investors should use it for good.

Embracing purposeful and productive actions and cultivating a culture of gratitude within the ecosystem initiates and propagates a virtuous cycle of positive karma. This cycle, in turn, generates an expansion of opportunities, collaborations, and growth. Embracing thanksgiving for these relationships and contributions strengthens the bonds of trust and camaraderie. Acknowledging and expressing gratitude for these relationships and contributions amplifies the positive energy, leading to beneficial business outcomes and motivating individuals to continue contributing their best to the community.

iii. Portfolio Diversification Creates an Ecosystem of Trust Bridges

By maintaining a diversified portfolio, investors at different stages can effectively mitigate risk while investing in a wide range of companies they are deeply passionate about and believe have the potential for a profitable future. Embracing innovation and disruption allows investors to diversify their investments across different stages, industries, technologies, and business models. This diversification strategy of building a portfolio of investments across multiple startups effectively helps mitigate the inherent risks associated with startup investing. It increases the chances of having successful investments that yield substantial returns. This approach allows investors to support various companies that align with their interests, values, and investment goals. By spreading their investments across various opportunities, investors can capture the potential for growth and innovation in different sectors while minimizing the impact of any single investment.

Diversifying their investments across a broad spectrum of companies, investors achieve more than risk mitigation; they also cultivate an extensive and varied network of trust and collaboration. This network allows for the exchange of knowledge, resources, and support, creating a synergistic environment where ideas, innovations, and opportunities can flow openly and freely; ultimately neutralizing bias that is inherent in the human condition. Through portfolio diversification, investors can build inclusive relationships with founders, industry experts, strategic partners, exit alliances, and fellow investors, cultivating a deeper sense of trust, acceptance, and credibility. These trust bridges enable the sharing of insights, experiences, and best practices, leading to collective learning and growth. Moreover, portfolio diversification encourages collaboration and co-investment, as investors can identify complementary strengths and align their resources to propel the narrative of innovation, insight, inclusion, and impact to nurture a robust and interconnected startup economy.

Chapter 6

The 5 M's for Startup Investing

Investing in startups is a high-risk proposition (have I said that enough?). These straightforward 5 M's offer investors the mindset and mental memory of the top aspects to consider in evaluating startups, helping to demystify typically complex and arduous evaluation. This simple framework (that's easy to remember even at a coffee meeting) can also jump-start the due diligence process with deeper dives into each concept with the founder(s), customers, or other investors. The appreciation and evaluation of a startup by an investor using the five fundamental principles play a pivotal role in determining the type and amount of capital an entrepreneur can secure. These principles serve as a crucial framework for investors to assess the potential of a startup and make informed funding decisions. Therefore, investors can focus on these 5 M's in evaluating any entrepreneurial venture: (1) Management, (2) Momentum, (3) Model, (4) Motivation, and (5) Market; with 2 bonus M's, Moat and Metrics. (Figure 5 – The 5 M's of Startup Investing)

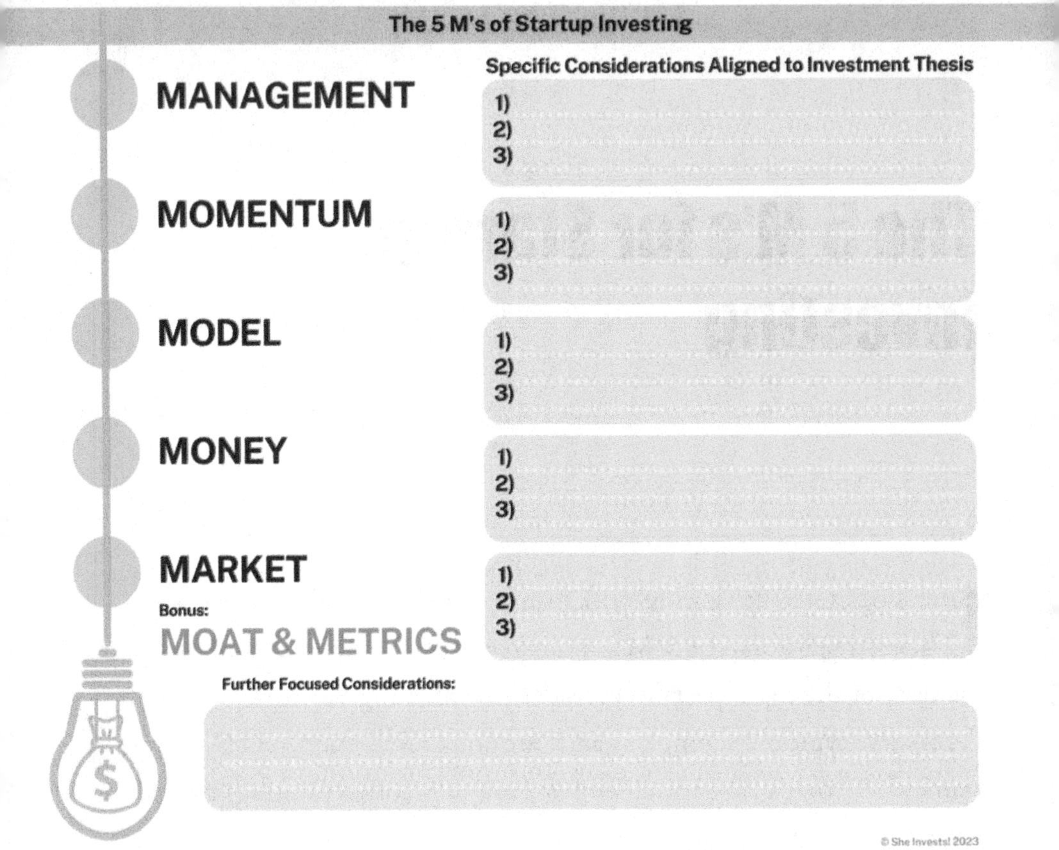

The 5 M's of Startup Investing

MANAGEMENT

MOMENTUM

MODEL

MONEY

MARKET

Bonus:
MOAT & METRICS

Specific Considerations Aligned to Investment Thesis
1)
2)
3)

Further Focused Considerations:

© She Invests! 2023

Figure 9

As an active investor, I consider these five concepts regularly when evaluating startups when casually speaking with a founder and asking them questions about their achievements, during pitch competitions (even if I am given a specific rubric for evaluation), championing a startup with another investor to consider funding, or conducting investor access/office hours. These 5 M's are also revisited by various angel groups, syndication networks, and angel conferences in analyzing startups for investment at the inception of the evaluation and continued due diligence process.

To overcome bias in the investment process, the 5 M's framework plays a crucial role by enabling investors to engage in promotion-focused conversations with founders rather than prevention-focused discussions. For example, promotion questions include, "Could you please clarify your competitive advantage to capture significant market share?" instead of a prevention question that would sound more like this, "How will you make it / stay relevant in this super crowded market?" Adopting this approach fosters a fair and unbiased process, thereby facilitating more in-depth analysis, promoting constructive dialogue, allowing for a more objective overall evaluation of startups, and fostering stronger working relationships with entrepreneurs. It also ensures that feedback remains constructive and avoids any unproductive negativity or emotional reactions. This method creates an environment where thoughtful and open conversations can flourish, devoid of personal and professional biases, leading to better outcomes and mutual understanding between investors and entrepreneurs.

Startups' valuations hold significant importance as they directly impact investment decisions and potential returns. Determining an appropriate valuation requires carefully assessing the startup's growth potential, market positioning, revenue generation, team expertise, and competitive advantage. Investors aim to strike a balance between investing at a reasonable valuation to maximize potential gains while minimizing risks associated with overvaluation. A startup with an attractive valuation may entice investors, but ensuring that the valuation aligns with its actual current value and growth prospects is crucial. Other considerations that can influence valuations when evaluating startups:

- ⊙ Industry (size, competitive landscape, and type of industry)
- ⊙ Startup stage (earlier stage have increased risk, thus lower valuations)
- ⊙ Geography (globalization has decreased this one, but still a factor)

- ⊘ Exit potential (attractiveness of potential exit and strengths are factors)
- ⊘ Market trends (growth, challenges, and disruption considerations)
- ⊘ Burn rate and runway (rate a startup spends cash and time to run out are factors)
- ⊘ Intellectual property defensibility (proprietary tech, patents, or unique know-how)
- ⊘ Customer base and revenue diversity (providing stability and reduce risk)
- ⊘ Team and execution (track record and traction increase investor confidence)

Moreover, valuations are not static and can evolve over time as the startup progresses through different stages of growth. Early-stage startups may have more speculative valuations, given the higher level of uncertainty and the potential for significant growth. As a startup achieves milestones, such as increasing revenues, expanding its customer base, or securing strategic partnerships, its valuation may increase, reflecting the growing potential and reduced risk. Seasoned investors carefully analyze these factors and engage in thorough due diligence to make informed decisions regarding valuations, with the ultimate goal of supporting startups with the most significant potential for success and generating attractive returns on investment.

At Stella Angels, we employ this analysis approach to facilitate discussions about startups that have recently pitched to us, enabling all members to provide their valuable insights and contribute purposefully. Our objective is to streamline the evaluation process and make it empowering, enhancing our ability to question and assess pitching startups collaboratively. We achieve this by adopting a framework that emphasizes a wholly promotion-focused approach, enabling us to support and uplift each other while providing valuable insights to the startups. By embracing simplicity and inclusivity, we aim to refine our evaluation techniques and foster a more supportive and growth-oriented environment. This framework ultimately allows for more individuals to participate and evaluate companies in a concise and efficient manner.

Investors seek the right team to scale the right company with the right customers for the right impact. From product-market fit to founder-market fit, investors must meticulously assess the complete evaluation of startups due to the inherent volatility and high-risk nature associated with early-stage investing. Investors seek startups that demonstrate scalability potential, a substantial and growing market, a sustainable competitive advantage, and a strong customer demand for their solutions, albeit B2B (Business-to-Business) or B2C (Business-to-Consumer). The 5 M's framework efficiently organizes the "why" and "how" of all crucial considerations, providing a succinct and user-friendly structure to distill the key factors behind investment decisions and easily share with other interested co-investors.

i. Management (the team)

The passion of the startup individual or team is contagious when it is genuinely communicated and embraced by all involved. Is the founder or founding team experienced enough to take this startup towards creating value inside the company (culture) and executing product deliverables? Is the founder coachable? Are there adequate scientific, technical, or industry advisors on the board who have validated the startup's potential and are fully supportive of its mission? How credible is the startup team? Is the investor confident in their ability to utilize investment funds effectively? How experienced are they in the industry they are going into? How experienced are they in creating startups?

Leadership plays a pivotal role in the eyes of investors, who prioritize founders with a genuine sense of empathy and dedication combined with a strong foundation of integrity and gratitude for the relationships, collaborations, and partnerships within their thriving ecosystem. Additionally, investors highly value a capable team that complements the founders, brings diverse expertise to the table, and exhibits a problem-solving mindset to navigate challenges and propel the company forward.

The tenacity and grit exhibited by startup founders have often been pivotal factors influencing investment decisions. A critical aspect that dramatically enhances the "founder-funder" connection is the character (or values) match between the entrepreneur and investor. Forging a robust and harmonious connection is paramount for achieving a meaningful return on investment, given the extensive time and collaboration that investors and entrepreneurs will share throughout the journey. The quality of this relationship significantly influences the overall outcome and performance of the investment, making it a crucial factor in the long-term success of the partnership.

ii. Momentum (traction)

Investors are drawn to founders who can demonstrate tangible progress and positive momentum or traction, as it reflects their ability to execute their vision effectively and overcome challenges. These momentum metrics can include revenue growth, customer acquisition, and retention rates, high MAU (Monthly Active Users) with a low CAC (Customer Acquisition Cost) and high LTV (Lifetime Value), funding from other investors, the establishment of strategic partners with strong LOIs (Letters of Intent) or MOUs (Memo/Memorandum of Understanding), completion of product development milestones, and positive feedback from early adopters or beta users. Additionally, showcasing triumphs and accolades within the immediate startup ecosystem and strong support from a network of mentors, advisors, and collaborators can be a powerful testament to the founder(s)' ability to attract experienced and influential individuals who believe in the startup's potential.

A non-stop attitude and relentless pursuit of their goals further indicate the founder's commitment and dedication to the venture. Traction can be a bit harder to evaluate at the earliest stages, but finding the seedlings of possible future traction is critical. For predicting revenues, pre-orders or sales of the startup's product indicate demand and early market interest. If the startup has received media coverage, whether it's through press releases, interviews, or features in publications, share these achievements to build credibility. High engagement, positive feedback, and insightful customer testimonials from early adopters indicate that the startup's product resonates with the target audience. In addition to traction illustrated through these metrics, founder(s) can showcase progress by presenting at conferences, engaging with angel investors (even informally over coffee), participating in startup events, or conducting customer interviews, all of which demonstrate positive progress towards growth.

iii. Model (show me the money)

The "Model" component of the 5 M's is a critical aspect that focuses on the startup's business model and how it envisions generating revenue. The startup founder(s) need to be able to clearly communicate how they expect to make money in the short and long term and orchestrate a profitable exit. Founder(s) should be crystal clear about the type of business model(s) employing: B2B (Business-to-Business), B2C (Business-to-Consumer), licensing, franchising, SAAS (Software as a Service), subscription-based, e-commerce, razor blade, or data monetization. These are just a few of the typical startup business models, but numerous other business models are tailored to specific industries, stages of business, and market dynamics.

Startups can employ various strategies to build their business models. Still, those that truly succeed are the ones that deeply understand the nuances of their industry and can innovate to create sustainable and profitable revenue streams that maximize returns for their stakeholders. A standout example of investing in a startup primarily because of its well-crafted business model is one that demonstrates the ability to create value and revenue even at an early stage, allowing for funding of the larger, long-term vision. This indicates a keen business acumen within the industry, highlighting the value of the investors' money and potential returns, as well as showcasing astute business model innovations.

iv. Motivation (why now?)

A significant market driver should form a fundamental aspect of the business model to establish a strong presence in a market. This market driver could stem from ripe industry technology, enabling a novel product delivery method (as exemplified by Zipline, a pioneering company operating drones within remote medical supply chains), or from customers' readiness to embrace innovative solutions within a flourishing sharing economy (akin to Radious, an online marketplace that transforms houses, apartments, and other residential properties into collaborative workspaces, available for rent daily). Capitalizing on the heightened market interest or seizing opportunities presented by cutting-edge technology becomes imperative to secure funding and launch a new venture.

Investors highly value the alignment between the entrepreneurial team and their product, especially when it runs in parallel with their passion and motivation for iterative design and successful commercialization. This synergy assures investors that the founders are not only dedicated to their vision but also possess the drive and adaptability required to maximize growth potential. The question of why this particular team is best suited to develop and execute the business model flawlessly for optimal proof of concept validation (and, ultimately, the startup's survival) is a critical consideration for investors. They seek assurance that the team possesses the necessary expertise, experience, and commitment to drive the venture forward. When the product aligns seamlessly with the team's expertise and the market's demands, it creates a compelling and sustainable value proposition.

Giving due consideration to Intellectual Property (IP) protection is imperative for ensuring long-term competitive advantage, particularly when it aligns with an opportune moment of commercialization in the market. Adequate IP safeguards can safeguard the uniqueness and innovation of the product, establishing a competitive advantage that endures in the market. The aspect of IP protection serves as a critical safeguard that shields the startup from easy replication by competitors, thereby reinforcing its market positioning and ensuring long-term sustainability. By securing exclusive rights to innovative ideas, products, or processes, the startup gains a competitive advantage that deters others from directly copying or imitating its offerings. This protection allows the startup to maintain its uniqueness, establish a distinct identity, and carve out a niche in the market. Additionally, IP protection enables the startup to capitalize on its creations without fear of unauthorized usage, piracy, or infringement, empowering it to invest in further research, development, and expansion confidently. As a result, the startup can confidently pursue its growth trajectory, confident in the knowledge that its intellectual assets are shielded, fostering continued innovation and success over time.

V. Market (are there enough customers to buy?)

When investors assess a funding opportunity, one of their primary considerations lies in analyzing the market size and growth potential. Startups that operate in expansive and burgeoning markets tend to attract significant attention from investors. Such markets offer a wealth of growth opportunities, making them appealing prospects for those seeking high returns on investment. The combination of a sizable market, significant market expansion potential, and the presence of growing market segments provide a compelling investment opportunity for investors. In addition, the startup's products have a substantial addressable market and the potential for scalability, allowing investors to envision the possibility of achieving impressive returns on their investment over time. As a result, startups demonstrating strong market potential become more likely to secure funding and garner the support needed to thrive in their industry.

The key considerations for evaluating the startup's market are:

- Assessing market size, particularly gauging the adequacy of the Total Addressable Market (TAM) to sustain the startup's growth aspirations and potential returns on investment
- Expanding the market growth rate is anchored on CAGR (Compounded Annual Growth Rate)
- Understanding of a clear need or problem for the specific target customer segment within the desired market

⊙ Evaluating a competitive landscape where the startup has significant competitive advantage and differentiation to determine its ability to capture market share

⊙ Demanding careful attention to the regulatory environment to assess impact on a startup's operations, either by creating favorable conditions that foster growth or by imposing barriers and challenges that hinder progress

Recognizing and capitalizing on favorable market trends, startups can leverage market opportunities, refine their offerings, and align their strategies to meet the demands of the ever-changing market. Market trends encompass shifts in consumer preferences, emerging technologies, evolving business models, and changing industry landscapes.

A typical early-stage VC would only look at a market of >> $500M, a growth rate of >> 10%, a large pain point among customers (in numbers/size of customers and value to the end-user), and a unique approach to solving pain.

When defining the market for a startup, two distinct strategies can be employed: the top-down and bottom-up methods. The top-down approach takes a macroeconomic perspective, examining factors such as market size, competitors, and overall industry trends. This method provides a broader and more comprehensive view of the market landscape.

Conversely, the bottom-up approach adopts a more granular perspective by delving into customer insights and estimating sales and adoption on a smaller scale with limited industry drivers. This method focuses on understanding the needs and preferences of potential customers and how the startup's offerings align with those demands.

By employing both the top-down and bottom-up approaches, startups can gain a well-rounded understanding of their target market. Leadership teams at startups, along with their trusted investors and advisors, can then make informed decisions and develop strategies that cater to the unique dynamics of the industry while meeting the specific needs of their customers.

vi. Bonus M's – Moat & Metrics

Alongside the 5 M's Framework, the moat and metrics components serve as essential guides and goalposts for making well-informed investment decisions. The concept of a moat revolves around identifying the startup's competitive advantage or unique value proposition, distinguishing it from its competitors in the market. Investors seek startups with a strong moat, whether through intellectual property, network effects, brand recognition, or other barriers to entry, as this enhances the startup's ability to sustain its competitive advantage in the market.

Investors analyze various financial and operational metrics to assess the startup's performance and potential for future success. This discovery includes revenue growth, customer acquisition costs, customer retention rates, gross margins, burn rate, and other key performance indicators. Vital and improving metrics, and the effective tracking of them by the startup's founding team, indicate the startup's ability to generate revenue, scale efficiently, and achieve profitability.

When investors rigorously apply these 5+2 principles to evaluate a startup, they are better equipped to make well-informed funding decisions. Entrepreneurs who effectively communicate their startup's strengths in alignment with these principles are more likely to secure the appropriate type and amount of capital they need to propel their venture forward. This correlation between comprehensive evaluation and positive funding outcomes underscores the importance of due diligence and strategic decision-making in the startup investment landscape.

Insights to Inspire Activation of Capital

Invention and innovation serve as the driving forces propelling the growth and progress of an economy, fostering creativity, and promoting capitalism. They fuel economic development, create jobs, and spur technological advancements across various industries. Entrepreneurs and inventors constantly strive to develop new ideas and products that meet the evolving needs of consumers and businesses. Startup investors catalyze innovation through investing.

The process of invention, innovation, impact, and investment is a tightly intricate synergistic feedback loop for the collective to thrive in their individual lanes of genius and strength. These interconnected elements create a dynamic ecosystem where each component reinforces and enhances the others. Invention and innovation foster a culture of entrepreneurship and risk-taking. Brilliantly, individuals and teams seek to disrupt traditional industries, introduce groundbreaking technologies, and find new market opportunities. This dynamic environment encourages competition, collaboration, and connectivity that ultimately requires and beguiles investment of financial capital, experiential capital, and network capital to be activated.

Investors, INVEST for character, TRUST in the team, BELIEVE in the innovation, and CREATE meaningful impact. Everything else can be learned, advised, and coached.

Passionately, innovation serves as the dynamic force propelling economic growth and elevating the very fabric of human existence. The relentless pursuit of innovation paves the way for advancements in healthcare, revolutionizes transportation, connects us seamlessly through communication, harnesses boundless energy, and transforms countless other domains. With each breakthrough, the quality of life for individuals and society at large ascends to new heights.

Beyond tangible progress, innovation holds the power to spark transformative change on a global scale. We can rise to confront and conquer the pressing challenges of our time through daring inventions and groundbreaking ideas. Climate change, poverty, and healthcare disparities loom as monumental hurdles, but the unwavering spirit of innovation offers the beacon of hope to navigate toward a brighter future.

From brilliant minds to collaborative efforts, the nature of invention drives us to explore uncharted territories, unraveling the mysteries of the universe and seeking solutions to age-old predicaments. It fuels the audacious dreamers and empowers the resilient doers to envision a world that knows no bounds.

In this ever-evolving journey of human ingenuity, investors stand witness to the limitless potential of innovation and entrepreneurship. It transcends barriers, defies norms, and shatters boundaries, ushering us toward a realm of infinite possibilities. As investors harness the transformative force of innovation, all embrace an existence enriched by progress, where the impact on lives is immeasurable, and the legacy of brilliance is etched forever.

Investment connectivity provides the necessary financial resources to support invention, innovation, and impact of the most extraordinary founders rooted in solid values and conviction along the entire funding continuum. Investments in research and development continue to commercialize pipelines, and business models drive sustainability. The founders' relentless determination, resilience, and willingness to bootstrap set the foundation for a startup's journey. With the steadfast support of friends and family, who believe in their vision, they gather the strength to take flight. Angel investors step in, providing the crucial wind beneath their wings, propelling them closer to their aspirations.

As the startup matures and dreams of exponential growth take shape, venture capitalists (VCs) come into the picture, sharing the belief in the company's potential and offering strategic guidance to navigate the skies of success. And when the time comes for a purposeful exit, investment bankers take the reins, infusing the journey with rocket fuel, propelling the startup towards its desired destination.

In this intricate dance of belief, support, and collaboration, a startup soars to great heights, soaring above challenges and seizing opportunities. This collective effort, the symphony of believers and enablers, fuels the entrepreneurial spirit, fostering innovation and transformation in the business landscape.

Together, these interconnected elements create a self-reinforcing cycle where invention drives innovation, which leads to impactful outcomes, attracting further investment. The continuous flow of resources and expertise fuels ongoing innovation that encourages more invention, creating a virtuous circle of economic growth and societal progress.

This guide was purposefully written to activate an investor's capital by embracing and adopting the startup investor mindset, a posture of growth, invention, development, and re-invention. Investing in startups can be emotionally and psychologically challenging. Investors can develop patience, discipline, and resilience by connecting with other investors, evaluating many startups in various investment opportunities, and creating a trusted pool of resources and advisors to support a flourishing portfolio while maintaining a long-term perspective. Investors lend gravity (anchor of support and funding) to the larger-than-life vision of most entrepreneurs.

I encourage readers who are investors to apply the principles, recommendations, and strategies discussed here to genuinely impact their startup ecosystems by confidently investing based on their unique investment thesis and, thus, building an intentionally diverse portfolio. In sharing these frameworks, lists, quotes, and insights, I aim to elevate investor awareness regarding the risks and rewards inherent in startup investing. I intended to keep it light, instructional from a strategic and tactical point of view, inspirational to increase hope, and with an appropriate level of rigor (I'm an academic and learner, so I cannot help myself). By providing valuable guidance, I aim to support investors in making more informed decisions, embarking on a well-traveled journey, and walking with similar intentional values amongst their own dynamic startup ecosystems around the globe.

To all the ambitious and bold entrepreneurs reading this guide, I sincerely wish that it has instilled in you a renewed sense of hope and possibility. May it serve as a reminder that some investors are genuinely aligned with your values, believe in the potential of your vision, and are eager to support your growth, joining you on the path to success. They understand the power of building networks and collaborations to benefit the entire ecosystem. Encourage them to get this guide to enhance their own strengths within the community. Embrace the journey with optimism.

For all the dedicated and hard-working community builders, including those who also serve as investors, I desire that this guide brings you renewed faith and inspiration. It is my sincere wish that this reinforces the importance of fostering a supportive and resourceful ecosystem where investors with a growth mindset and entrepreneurs creating mindful products can come together. Stay committed to your journey, knowing that your efforts, your intricate DNA, are guided by your inherent values and the desire to make a positive impact. I am one of you; we do the good, hard work. Stay the course; your north star shines bright in the constellation of entrepreneurs, investors, and others we call "familia" (or family).

If you found this guide helpful, I would appreciate it if you could let me know and share your feedback. It would also be fantastic and wonderful if you could spread the word within your network, allowing others to benefit from the insights and ideas shared. Remember, true wealth lies in the growth, positivity, grace, and mindset we collectively cultivate, created by innovation, impact, and investment of the entire startup ecosystem.

Frequently Asked Questions

i. Does product-market fit hold significance for investment evaluations?

Product-market fit has tactical relevance in the process of sourcing and reviewing specific startups for potential investment (and a whole book could be written about this exact question). While product-market fit is highly desirable for a startup, as an early-stage investor, the evaluation and funding decisions may occur before the startup achieves true product-market fit. However, attaining product-market fit, where the startup has a validated product and enthusiastic customers in a thirsty market highly receptive to the startup's offering, becomes a significant green flag. Various indicators and milestones within the industry can be used to demonstrate progress toward achieving product-market fit. These can include early customer interest evidenced by customer interviews, initial revenue generation for consumer packaged goods (CPG), or letters of intent (LOI) from business-to-business (B2B) customers. As an investor, it's essential to evaluate the startup's trajectory toward product-market fit and assess the potential for achieving it in the near future. By keeping an eye on these signals, investors can make informed decisions and support startups that have the potential to reach their full market potential.

ii. Is founder-market fit an important consideration for investors?

This term "founder-market fit" carries a level of ambiguity, has gained significant prominence, and requires a deeper understanding. It goes beyond evaluating the product or idea; it delves into the very core of the entrepreneurial journey. Investors recognize that founders who possess a deep passion, a strong alignment, and an understanding of the industries they aim to disrupt or innovate in are better equipped. Founder-market fit also fosters credibility and trust with stakeholders, including customers, partners, and investors. When founders can genuinely communicate their passion and knowledge, it enhances their ability to attract strategic partnerships for growth.

Founder-market fit revolves around visionary entrepreneurs who possess an innate comprehension of a specific strategic advantage within a market. It is the seamless fusion of their expertise, past experiences, and personal motivations, all harmoniously aligned with the particular market they are targeting. This profound connection with the market breathes life into their understanding of the customers they serve, enabling them to cater to their needs with unmatched empathy and insight.

In essence, founder-market fit embodies the profound harmony between the entrepreneur's skills and aspirations and the unique demands and dynamics of the market they choose to conquer. Such expertise allows them to navigate complexities, identify unique solutions, and build meaningful connections with potential customers, partners, and stakeholders. When founders have a genuine connection to the problem they are trying to solve, it creates an authenticity and drive that can impact the specific mindful direction of the startup, laser-focused on the exact competitive advantage. This intimate understanding of the market dynamics and pain points fosters a stronger vision and strategy, inspiring investor confidence.

Note to reader: The essence of this guide lies in its wide accessibility and utility, intended to be embraced and employed by numerous investors, mentors, advisors, and entrepreneurs alike. With each successive edition, this section remains dynamic, continually evolving through the inclusion of fresh insights, thoughtful inquiries, and innovative perspectives contributed by a diverse array of brilliant startup investors. As a living resource, it thrives on the collective wisdom and experiences of the community, enriching the journeys of those who embark on the path of startup investing.

Resources

Carlson, E. R., & Tannyhill, R. J. (2020). The Growth Mindset: A Contextualization of Faculty Development. *Journal of Oral and Maxillofacial Surgery, 78*(1), 7–9. https://doi.org/10.1016/j.joms.2019.07.020

Dweck, C. (2012). *Mindset: Changing The Way You Think To Fulfill Your Potential.* Hachette UK.

FutureLearn. (2022). Updates, Insights, and News from FutureLearn | Online Learning for You. *FutureLearn.* https://www.futurelearn.com/info/courses/developing-curiosity/0/steps/156381

Gurteen, D. (1998). Knowledge, Creativity, and Innovation. *Journal of Knowledge Management, 2*(1), 5–13. https://doi.org/10.1108/13673279810800744

Blank, S. (2022, January 3). Why the Lean Start-Up Changes Everything. Harvard Business Review. https://hbr.org/2013/05/why-the-lean-start-up-changes-everything

Anthony, S. D. (2022, July 28). 3 Ways to Innovate in a Downturn. Harvard Business Review. https://hbr.org/2022/07/3-ways-to-innovate-in-a-downturn

Patel, N. (2015b, January 16). 90% Of Startups Fail: Here's What You Need To Know About The 10%. Forbes.

https://www.forbes.com/sites/neilpatel/2015/01/16/90-of-startups-will-fail-heres-what-you-need-to-know-about-the-10

Spigel, B. (2017). The Relational Organization of Entrepreneurial Ecosystems. *Entrepreneurship Theory and Practice, 41*(1), 49–72. https://doi.org/10.1111/etap.12167

Coyne, K. (2014, August 1). Taking the Mystery Out of Investor Behavior. Harvard Business Review. https://hbr.org/2002/09/taking-the-mystery-out-of-investor-behavior

The new roles of leaders in 21st century organizations. (2019, September 23). McKinsey & Company. https://www.mckinsey.com/capabilities/people-and-organizational-performance/our-insights/the-organization-blog/the-new-roles-of-leaders-in-21st-century-organizations

Brand Archetypes & How They Can Help Your Business | The Hartford. (n.d.). https://www.thehartford.com/business-insurance/strategy/brand-archetypes/choosing-brand-archetype

Bhidé, A. (2022, April 19). The Questions Every Entrepreneur Must Answer. Harvard Business Review. https://hbr.org/1996/11/the-questions-every-entrepreneur-must-answer

Cholakova, M., & Clarysse, B. (2015). Does the Possibility to Make Equity Investments in Crowdfunding Projects Crowd Out Reward–Based Investments? *Entrepreneurship Theory and Practice, 39*(1), 145–172. https://doi.org/10.1111/etap.12139

Feldman, S. (2023b). Companies buying companies: The different types and methods of mergers and acquisitions. *www.wolterskluwer.com*. https://www.wolterskluwer.com/en/expert-insights/the-different-types-and-methods-of-mergers-and-acquisitions

Nanda, R., & Rhodes-Kropf, M. (2013). Investment cycles and startup innovation. *Journal of Financial Economics, 110*(2), 403–418. https://doi.org/10.1016/j.jfineco. 2013.07.001

A History of Silicon Valley. (n.d.). https://www.scaruffi.com/svhistory/arun3.html

Voices, V. (2018, September 14). Is Pattern Recognition Killing Innovation? Forbes. https://www.forbes.com/sites/valleyvoices/2018/09/14/pattern-recognition-killing-innovation

Miles, B. (2017). *#BreakIntoVC: How to Break Into Venture Capital and Think Like an Investor Whether You're a Student, Entrepreneur, Or Working Professional.*

Hudson, M. (2018, August 8). The Rewards of Being an Angel Investor. (n.d.). https://www.angelcapitalassociation.org/blog/the-rewards-of-being-an-angel-investor/

Kersten, A., & Athanasia, G. (2022, December 9). Addressing the Gender Imbalance in Venture Capital and Entrepreneurship. https://www.csis.org/analysis/addressing-gender-imbalance-venture-capital-and-entrepreneurship.

Huang, Laura, Andy Wu, Min Ju Lee, Jiayi Bao, Marianne Hudson, and Elaine Bolle. "The American Angel: The First In-Depth Report on the Demographics and Investing Activity of Individual American Angel Investors." Report, Overland Park, KS, November 2017.

Patel, D. (2018, May 16). 8 Negotiating Tactics Every Successful Entrepreneur Has Mastered. *Entrepreneur.* https://www.entrepreneur.com/growing-a-business/8-negotiating-tactics-every-successful-entrepreneur-has/312685

Berkowitz, B. (2021, November 18). *10 Characteristics of Truly Great VCs*. (n.d.). https://www.goingvc.com/post/10-characteristics-of-truly-great-vcs

Clarke, C. (2020, September 19). BIPOC: What does it mean and where does it come from? CBS News. https://www.cbsnews.com/news/bipoc-meaning-where-does-it-come-from-2020-04-02/

Porter, M. E. (1980). *Competitive Strategy: Techniques for Analyzing Industries and Competitors*. New York : Free Press ; Toronto : Maxwell Macmillan Canada.

Christensen, C. (2013). *The Innovator's Dilemma: When New Technologies Cause Great Firms to Fail*. Harvard Business Review Press.

Brown, L. (2015, May 26). *The Importance of Developing Curiosity*. Psych Central. https://psychcentral.com/blog/the-importance-of-developing-curiosity#2

Baer, D., & Hoque, F. (2014). *Everything Connects: How to Transform and Lead in the Age of Creativity, Innovation, and Sustainability*. McGraw-Hill Education.

LPC, D. C. P. M. (2015c, February 21). *Understand the Difference: Creativity vs. Artistic Ability*. Psych Central. https://psychcentral.com/blog/unleash-creativity/2015/02/creativity-vs-artistic-ability

StartupCincy. (2023, March 17). *Resources - StartupCincy*. https://startupcincy.com/resources1/

SEC.gov | HOME. (2017, February 5). https://www.sec.gov/

SEC.gov | Frequently asked questions about exempt offerings. (2017, May 5). https://www.sec.gov/education/smallbusiness/exemptofferings/faq

Gallup, Inc. (2023, June 28). *CliftonStrengths Online Talent Assessment |*
EN - Gallup. Gallup.com.
https://www.gallup.com/cliftonstrengths

Ravishankar, R. A. (2022, August 30). *5 Ways to Set More Achievable*
Goals. Harvard Business Review. https://hbr.org/2022/08/5-
ways-to-set-more-achievable-goals

Sull, D. (2018, June 5). *With Goals, FAST Beats SMART.* MIT Sloan
Management Review. https://sloanreview.mit.edu/article/with-
goals-fast-beats-smart/

Hopper, G. (2023, March 21). Private Equity Vs. Venture Capital: Which
Is Right For Your Startup? *Forbes.*
https://www.forbes.com/sites/forbesfinancecouncil/2023/03/21
/private-equity-vs-venture-capital-which-is-right-for-your-startup

Carlson, C. R. (2020, November 18). *Innovation for Impact.* Harvard
Business Review. https://hbr.org/2020/11/innovation-for-
impact

Zider, B. (2023, April 24). *How Venture Capital Works.* Harvard Business
Review. https://hbr.org/1998/11/how-venture-capital-works

Kanze, D. (2021, September 17). *Male and Female Entrepreneurs Get*
Asked Different Questions by VCs — and It Affects How Much
Funding They Get. Harvard Business Review.
https://hbr.org/2017/06/male-and-female-entrepreneurs-get-
asked-different-questions-by-vcs-and-it-affects-how-much-
funding-they-get

Kerpen, C. (2018, April 9). *How Women Entrepreneurs Are Closing The*
Venture Capital Gap. Forbes.
https://www.forbes.com/sites/carriekerpen/2018/04/09/how-
women-entrepreneurs-are-closing-the-venture-capital-gap

Investor Journal

Investor Journal Entry #1. What characteristics of the startup investor mindset did I activate today?

....

....

....

....

....

....

....

....

....

....

....

....

....

....

....

Journaling Molds Mindsets

Investor Journal Entry #2. What positive beliefs did I embrace today when evaluating a startup to invest in?

....

....

....

....

....

....

....

....

....

....

....

....

....

....

....

....

....

....

Mindset Mantras drive Impact

Investor Journal Entry #3. I invest in startup founders who believe

....

....

....

....

....

....

....

....

....

....

....

....

....

....

....

....

....

....

....

Investor Journal Entry #4. What insights did I gain from a startup ecosystem activity I engaged with?

....

....

....

....

....

....

....

....

....

....

....

....

....

....

....

....

....

Build a Strong Network to Grow Your Networth

About the Author

Dr. Silvia Mah | Igniting Innovation, Impact & Investing through Action & Intentionality | VC | Keynote Speaker | Advocate 4 Diverse Founders | Investor | Published Author | Servant Leader

Dr. Silvia Mah is General Partner at Stella Impact Capital, a seed-stage venture fund, investing in diverse women founders building scalable startups at the intersection of deep tech & impact.

Focused on "Impact with Integrity", Dr. Mah is the founder & Chairwoman of Stella Foundation, founder of the startup accelerator Stella Labs, and Founding Investor Member of Stella Angels, all contributing to a national conSTELLAtion of organizations and leaders walking alongside women-led businesses from startup to sale and the funders who champion them.

Dr. Silvia Mah is also a redemptive entrepreneur and investor serving as the Director of Innovationand Adjunct Professor at the Crowell Business School at Biola University. As an active venture capitalist, Dr. Mah has also served as Investment Committee member of Next Wave Impact, a social impact venture fund; the inaugural Fund Manager for the San Diego Angel Conference Fund I (2019), and co-fund manager for Funds

II (2020), III (2021), IV (2022), and V (2023), an angel fund to activate regional & global capital from aspiring and existing angel investors; and a founding partner of Ad Astra Ventures.

Since 2010, Dr. Mah has invested in over 140+ seed-stage startups that are female-led or have BIPOC founders, from medical devices to life sciences to SAAS platforms to CPG companies and from San Diego, Portland and Brooklyn. Dr. Mah is honored to have also invested in 11 emerging fund managers and has been blessed by 6 exits and 1 IPO.

Dr. Mah holds a Ph.D. in Marine Molecular Biology from UC San Diego Scripps Institution of Oceanography, an M.B.A. from UC San Diego Rady School of Management, and a B.S. in Biology with Honors from Pepperdine University.

When not working, Dr. Mah enjoys sunny beaches, Disney days, & off-roading with her husband and 3 children in San Diego. Originally from Caracas, Venezuela, Dr. Mah believes in integrating family and work to create a lifestyle that serves both with a strong cup of integrity.

Made in the USA
Columbia, SC
06 September 2023

22483856R00076